on track ...
Magnum

every album, every song

Matthew Taylor

sonicbondpublishing.com

Sonicbond Publishing Limited
www.sonicbondpublishing.co.uk
Email: info@sonicbondpublishing.co.uk

First Published in the United Kingdom 2024
First Published in the United States 2024

British Library Cataloguing in Publication Data:
A Catalogue record for this book is available from the British Library

ISBN 978-1-78952-286-0

Typeset in ITC Garamond Std & ITC Avant Garde Gothic
Printed and bound in England

Graphic design and typesetting: Full Moon Media

Follow us on social media:
Twitter: https://twitter.com/SonicbondP
Instagram: www.instagram.com/sonicbondpublishing_/
Facebook: www.facebook.com/SonicbondPublishing/

Linktree QR code:

on track ...

Magnum

Contents

Would you like to write for Sonicbond Publishing?
At Sonicbond Publishing we are always on the look-out for authors,
particularly for our two main series:

On Track. Mixing fact with in depth analysis, the On Track series examines
the work of a particular musical artist or group. All genres are considered
from easy listening and jazz to 60s soul to 90s pop, via rock and metal.

On Screen. This series looks at the world of film and television. Subjects
considered include directors, actors and writers, as well as entire television
and film series. As with the On Track series, we balance fact with analysis.

While professional writing experience would, of course, be an advantage
the most important qualification is to have real enthusiasm and knowledge
of your subject. First-time authors are welcomed, but the ability to write
well in English is essential.

Sonicbond Publishing has distribution throughout Europe and North
America, and all books are also published in E-book form. Authors will be
paid a royalty based on sales of their book.

Further details are available from www.sonicbondpublishing.co.uk. To
contact us, complete the contact form there or
email info@sonicbondpublishing.co.uk

Introduction

On 10 December 2022, Magnum celebrated their 50th anniversary with a special Christmas concert at KK's Steel Mill in Wolverhampton. The setlist reflected the band's long history as a staple of British hard rock. It featured 16 songs drawn from eleven albums from 1978 up to 2022, with all but one of the band's six-decade existence being represented.

Spanning the late-1970s tail end of the first wave of prog rock and hard rock and into the so-called New Wave of British Heavy Metal (NWOBHM) period of the 1980s, and then operating at the margins of late 1980s hair metal, Magnum was always something of an outsider band that never quite fitted into any musical category. Variously described as 'pomp rock', 'progressive rock', 'heavy rock', 'melodic rock', and, more recently, simply as 'classic rock', the band was difficult to pigeonhole from the start, which may go some way towards explaining why they never quite made it commercially to the top tier of British rock, despite enjoying Gold and Silver album sales, Top-40 singles, and selling out large arena venues in the UK during the late 1980s.

Yet it is precisely the range and versatility of the band's material, as well as the quality and consistency of guitarist Tony Clarkin's songwriting, that helps us to understand why the band has maintained such a loyal and devoted fanbase across five decades. In March 2022, Get Ready to Rock radio broadcast a series of programmes celebrating 'Magnum Month', which included fans, critics and even former band members reflecting on the question: 'What Magnum Means to Me?' The responses from fans underlined the importance of the band's music in providing a backdrop to their emotional ups and downs but also the close connections that were forged between Magnum and its followers back in the 1980s and have been maintained ever since. As one put it: 'Like thousands of others, Magnum has provided the soundtrack to my life, good times and bad times and are one of the few bands that truly engage with their fans!'

Magnum emerged in Birmingham around 1972 from the collaboration of vocalist Bob Catley and guitarist Tony Clarkin, both already established figures in the city's 'Brum Beat' music scene. Born in Aldershot, Hampshire, on 11 September 1947, Catley's family moved to Birmingham when he was young. He initially worked for the General Post Office (GPO) but soon developed his musical interests and joined a series of local bands during the 1960s, including The Smokestacks and The Capitol Systems, who then changed their name to Paradox (and also featured early Magnum bassist Dave Morgan). Catley achieved limited success with Paradox, releasing a single in 1969 called 'Goodbye Mary' on Mercury Records.

Clarkin, meanwhile, born 24 November 1946 in the Shard End area of Birmingham, had been a ladies' hairdresser on leaving school but formed his first band in around 1964. Called The Boulevards, it consisted of Clarkin's former schoolmates and was influenced in its early days by Cliff Richard

5

and the Shadows, Elvis Presley and Buddy Holly before incorporating blues and then soul influences. The guitarist was evidently inspired by the musicians he saw and came into contact with at the time. He recalls, in Laurie Hornsby's *Brum Rocked On!*, 'watching every guitar lick [Pat Wayne and the Beachcombers guitarist] Geoff Roberts put down' and apparently after hearing tales of 'the antics of a professional band on the road' from another visiting musician, Clarkin admitted to '[telling] the lads there and then that I'd got to have some of that no matter what!'

The Boulevards split in late 1966 and Clarkin and rhythm guitarist/bassist Ken Picket joined Hemel Hempstead band The Question, from whom bassist John Lodge had just left to join The Moody Blues. For the next few years, Clarkin played in various bands with a number of musicians prominent in the 'Brum Beat' scene, including former The Move and The Uglys and future Electric Light Orchestra (ELO) keyboardist Richard Tandy.

Although Catley and Clarkin knew each other from the local scene, it wasn't until 1972 that they started playing together. Catley was lead singer with Fred's Box, a resident band at the Rum Runner nightclub on Broad Street in Birmingham. On the drums was Kevin 'Kex' Gorin (born 1 January 1949), another Shard End native who had previously played with Catley in The Smokestacks as well as The Andicaps, the first band founded by Jeff Lynne, later famous as a member of The Move and co-founder and leader of ELO. It was Gorin who approached Clarkin to join the band in a line-up completed by bassist Bob Doyle, who was later replaced by 'Brum Beat' veteran Dave Morgan.

Nobody seems to know precisely when the name Magnum was adopted. Martin Vielhaber's online biography of the band suggests that the idea came from the mother of first guitarist Les Kitcheridge, who suggested naming the group after the double-sized champagne bottles. Catley's claim in a 2022 *Record Collector* interview that the name was inspired by the champagne bottles at the Rum Runner lends support to this view, although in his autobiography, Morgan suggested that the name came from Clarkin and was inspired by the powerful gun associated with films such as Clint Eastwood's *Dirty Harry* (and its pertinently titled sequel *Magnum Force*).

Whatever the case, Magnum's time as a resident band playing chart hits at the Rum Runner was numbered when they began to introduce some of Clarkin's own compositions into the set. As Catley recalled: 'We were fed up with what we were doing, but we forgot what we were there for: for people to dance to'. The band were duly sacked and found themselves at a loose end, making money doing sessions where they could. They toured the UK, supporting such high-profile names as Del Shannon and soul singer Eddie Holman. They also established a residency at The Railway pub on Curzon Street, where they developed their stagecraft and honed Clarkin's tunes. By this point, Morgan had left to be replaced by Colin 'Wally' Lowe, while keyboardist and flautist Richard Bailey re-joined in late 1976, having been a member for a short time in 1973.

This was the line-up that signed to Jet Records and recorded *Kingdom Of Madness* (1978), *Magnum II* (1979) and live album *Marauder* (1980). Local keyboardist Mark Stanway replaced Bailey for 1982's breakthrough *Chase The Dragon* and *The Eleventh Hour* (1983). But poor promotion and disappointing record sales, along with a serious illness afflicting Clarkin, led to a low point around 1983-84, with band members leaving and rumours of a split.

Nonetheless, Clarkin and new manager Keith Baker pulled the band together for 1985's *On A Storyteller's Night*, which ushered in the second and most commercially successful phase of their career. Signing to a major label, Polydor, Magnum released *Vigilante* (1986) and *Wings Of Heaven* (1988), from which three singles were selected and went Top 40. The final album with Polydor was the controversial US-recorded *Goodnight LA,* after which the band's popularity stalled in the grunge and then Britpop-obsessed 1990s with the release of *Sleepwalking* (1992) and *Rock Art* (1994).

Clarkin split the band up in 1995, but he and Catley stayed together to record two albums under a new name, Hard Rain. Not long after Catley left to concentrate on a solo career, Clarkin wound up Hard Rain and decided in 2001 to resurrect the Magnum moniker, bringing in Hard Rain bassist Al Barrow and former Thunder drummer Harry James to join him, Catley and Stanway in a reformed line-up.

The reunion phase of Magnum's career has so far produced an impressive 12 studio, four live and three compilation albums. While there have been peaks and valleys in the fortunes of the band, the overall trajectory has been upwards, with 2018's *Lost On The Road To Eternity* achieving the first UK Top-20 chart entry since 1990 and national radio airplay. Stability has also been a feature of the reunion phase, with the line-up staying consistent up until the departures of Stanway in 2016, James in 2017 and Barrow in 2019. Magnum have also established an excellent relationship with German label SPV, who have released all of the band's post-reunion albums, and generally leave Clarkin free to write and produce the records he wants.

Dismissed even in the 1980s as grizzled veterans, Clarkin and Catley continued to produce and perform inventive, expansive and intelligent music well into their mid-seventies. While it may be something of a cliché to say so, there's nonetheless no doubt that Magnum are among the most underrated bands in British rock history. Their story and their music deserve to be better known.

Kingdom Of Madness (1978)

Personnel:
Tony Clarkin: all guitars and backing vocals
Bob Catley: vocals
Richard Bailey: all keyboards, flute and backing vocals
Colin 'Wally' Lowe: bass guitar and backing vocals
Kex Gorin: drums
Additional musicians:
Dave Morgan: bass guitar on the Nest Demos and 1975 'Sweets For My Sweet'
single; lead vocals on 'Sweets For My Sweet' and (possibly) 'Baby I Need'
Produced at De Lane Lea Studios, London, by Jake Commander
Engineers: Dick Plant, Barry Kidd and Dave Strickland
Release date: 2 August 1978 on Jet Records
Cover Design: Original US cover by Stewart Daniels; Original UK Iris cover
by David Pilton Advertising Limited; re-released 1998 album cover by Rodney
Matthews
Highest chart places: UK: 58, West Germany and Sweden: Did not chart
Running time: 39:41

The story of Magnum's debut album really began around 1975, when Tony
Clarkin and then-bassist Dave Morgan, became involved in construction work
on a recording studio in Birmingham. In return for their labour, the band
were given studio time to record demos that were passed on to Jet Records,
possibly via the influence of Jeff Lynne, a friend of Clarkin's, whose band,
ELO, were signed to Jet. The label liked the demos, signed the band and
booked them into the prestigious De Lane Lea Studios in London, where
The Rolling Stones, The Who, Jimi Hendrix and Queen had all previously
recorded. As Clarkin told the *Birmingham Evening Mail* at the time: 'We
sent Jet some tapes and they said: "Do an album". It was as casual as that'.
However, the relationship with Jet seems to have been strained from the
beginning. The band had to sleep in the foyer of the studio because the hotel
the label had booked was so poor; when they were moved to a better hotel, it
was clear that Jet had unsettled bills there, too.

The initial De Lane Lea sessions took place in 1976, but it was another
two years before the *Kingdom Of Madness* album was finally released.
The reasons for the delay are not entirely clear. A 1988 *Metal Hammer*
interview referred to a 'series of insurmountable problems, inexplicable
to this day and typical of Magnum's association with the Jet label'. A more
precise explanation, outlined in press reports at the time of the album's
release, is that the delay resulted from prolonged legal problems related to a
management deal the band wanted to be freed from.

Whatever the reason, the long delay gave Clarkin the chance to write new
material that reshaped the final album. The guitarist's affection for British
and American progressive rock bands such as Yes and Kansas may well have

been an impetus for the development of more complex material, while tours supporting bands such as Judas Priest in 1977 surely helped to harden the sound. Three newer songs, including opener 'In The Beginning' were recorded during an intense 36-hour session, replacing 'some of the lighter tunes' from the original recordings, such as 'Find The Time', 'Without Your Love', 'Everybody Needs' and 'Master Of Disguise', on the final album. In an October 1978 interview, *Sounds*' Geoff Barton interpreted the album as 'a mixture of songs from two projected LPs, the fairly straight-ahead material from the first being mixed with "loosely conceptual" numbers from the second'.

In spite of this, the album, produced by Jake Commander, a friend of the band and Jeff Lynne's guitar roadie, is fairly cohesive. This is aided by the fact that most of the songs segue into each other and are presented as a comprehensible entity even though there's no clear conceptual unity. Clarkin noted in 1988 that he still looked at the tracks 'Kingdom Of Madness' and 'In The Beginning' 'with real fondness' despite the 'aerie-fairie' subject matter and some 'duffo' sounds. More recently, he has distanced himself from this and the other Jet albums, remarking that he hasn't listened to them for decades. However, *Kingdom Of Madness* was well-reviewed at the time, particularly by the aforementioned Geoff Barton. He gave the album four stars in *Sounds*, comparing it to bands such as Styx, Kansas, Yes, Queen and Starcastle and applauding the '[t]itanically powerful musical passages and soft, subtle acoustic interludes [that] combine to create an LP of great stature'.

It is the intricacy and diversity of *Kingdom Of Madness* that sets it apart from anything else in the Magnum catalogue. The progressive influences – from both sides of the Atlantic – were more pronounced here than they were to become. Clarkin noted in the sleeve notes to the 2005 reissue that at this time, he was trying to 'draw pictures' with his songs: 'In those days, I looked at music a bit like an animated film'. Yet it was also a record with a strong melodic spine and a keen understanding of the interaction between the lighter and heavier elements of the band's emerging sound. While the material was to become more consistent on subsequent albums, Magnum were never able to reproduce the quirky personality of this debut album.

Kingdom Of Madness has boasted a number of different album sleeves. The original US version featured an illustration by the American artist Stewart Daniels, who worked for Jet as well as other labels like Motown and Warner Brothers. A literal interpretation of the album title, it depicts food and furniture flying from the banquet table of a seemingly crazed monarch. For the UK, Jet used a more restrained black sleeve showing a close-up eye with a colourful depiction of a medieval city in the iris. Designed by David Picton advertising, this became the standard sleeve. FM's 1998 reissue came with a third cover – a Rodney Matthews illustration called 'The Dwarves Of Belegost' based on an episode in Tolkien's *The Silmarillion* that has little obvious connection to the theme of the album.

With few exceptions, Tony Clarkin has been the sole songwriter for Magnum throughout their career. Thus, all songs are written by Clarkin unless indicated.

'In The Beginning' (7:52)

The first song on the debut album is as prog rock as Magnum ever got. It was a bold idea to open with a complex, multi-part piece rather than one of their more conventional rock tunes. But 'In The Beginning' is brilliant stuff; a winding, melodic colossus of a track that sounds dated and a bit daft at times, yet still mesmerises.

A song in three parts, it opens with a brief twin guitar and keyboard introduction before phased synths and acoustic guitar give way after 44 seconds to a busy, ringing keyboard phrase reminiscent of Genesis and Yes. Mark Kelly was probably also listening as the sound is not unlike elements of early Marillion. There's another catchy keyboard riff before Catley's wordy vocals come in and take the song up another notch. Although Bailey is the dominant force in this section – with melodies and counter melodies crossing and intersecting – Clarkin makes his presence felt with a warm Thin Lizzy-style twin guitar break at 2.26.

The 'Prince Of Dreams' section, arriving at 4.15, is mellower, with acoustic guitar and spacey synth effects. Slightly buried in the mix in the first movement, Clarkin comes to the fore with an expressive performance here. A tight rhythm unit also ensures that the song's shifting moods and dynamics flow naturally. Strummed acoustic guitar at 6.52 presages the final sprint to the finish. Clarkin lets rip with a brief solo; there's an even briefer reprise of the opening bars of the song, then some backward recording, vocal improvisations, and an echoing chant of 'Madness' (hinting at the forthcoming title song) to bring things to a close.

'In The Beginning' is a fabulous slice of prog-rock Magnum style. There may be too many ideas crammed into nearly eight minutes, but the song maintains a coherence that some contemporaries struggled to achieve. Lyrically, it has tended to be dismissed as other-worldly, fantasy fare, but there's also a strong strain of Christian imagery, from the title through to references to the 'prince of dreams', 'prophet of the morning star' and the final 'I am your light/I am your god given light'.

An edited version cutting out the entire 'Prince Of Dreams' section was released on the reverse of the 'Kingdom Of Madness' single.

'Baby Rock Me' (4:05)

Oh dear! From the brilliantly conceived, bombastic opening track, we move on to possibly the worst song in the entire Magnum catalogue. 'Baby Rock Me' is just awful. Quite how this sub-standard, Queen-soundalike slice of boogie rock made it onto the album ahead of some of the superior culled songs from the 1976 album session, such as 'Master Of Disguise' and

'Everybody Needs', is hard to fathom. It certainly wasn't down to the lyrics, which are appalling, misogynistic nonsense even by the low standards of the mid-1970s. The second verse is especially pitiful: 'Now if you're looking to please/Well, then that's all I need/But when you're giving me head/ Remember what I said'.

Bizarrely, it was released (with 'Universe' on the B-side) as a single in the US sometime in 1978 and was resuscitated to act as a B-side to *Magnum II*'s 'Foolish Heart' a full year later.

'Universe' (3:45)

In contrast to the two numbers that proceed it, 'Universe' is a soothing, gentle song highlighting the diversity of moods present across the debut album. It's a track dominated by Bailey's keyboard concoctions – the spacey synth introduction as well as the soft rock keyboards. Lowe's bass work is also impressive here, pushed high in the mix and working in tandem with Gorin's appropriately languid drumming. Buttressed by a simple but effective melody delivered with control and feeling by Catley, it's not surprising that 'Universe' was chosen as the album's second single (backed by 'Invasion'), although, like the title track, it made no impression whatsoever on the UK charts.

'Kingdom Of Madness' (4:25)

The diversity of the album is encapsulated in the title track. Part heavy rock, part prog and part folk whimsy, 'Kingdom Of Madness' represents an early creative milestone for Magnum as well as a superbly realised 1970s rock classic. It begins with a lovely picked acoustic guitar pattern which is soon accompanied by Bailey's mysterious flute refrain. At 37 seconds, a simple staccato guitar riff cuts in and we seem to be in proto-metal territory as Catley weaves a fantastical tale of 'dreams', 'whirlpools' and 'seas of fire'. It's an incredibly powerful piece of writing that has surely sunken itself into the consciousness of a good many heavy rock fans of the era and may be one of the reasons why Magnum became somewhat erroneously associated with the burgeoning NWOBHM scene in the early 1980s.

The band's control over light and shade is evident in the transitions between the driving metallic riff and the acoustically-infused chorus. With birdsong and pastoral sound effects, the middle eight seems to offer the narrator some calming respite from the chaotic 'madness' depicted in the rest of the song. However, there's a sting in the tale as we're told twice that 'everyone's laughing' but then that 'everyone's laughing but me'. If the references to 'minstrels' and 'jesters' were a bit clichéd even at the time, it's nonetheless difficult not to smile at the confidence with which the band carry the whole thing off.

'Kingdom Of Madness' is the one track from the debut album that has remained a firm live favourite throughout the band's career. Live versions have generally left out the acoustic introduction, while both the 1978 single edit, and an alternate version recorded at Battle Studios in Hastings in 1979 omitted it entirely. This is a shame; while the live take has been harder and heavier, it has also invariably been less intricate and interesting than its studio cousin. The band rested the song for a couple of tours during the late 1980s and early 1990s due to Clarkin, in particular, becoming bored of playing it. But it remains the only Magnum song to be played live in each decade since the 1970s.

'All That Is Real' (3:48)
Side two of the vinyl begins with this pleasant tune featuring lush keyboard soundscapes tied down by a crisp Lowe bass line. The first half of the track is more soft than hard rock, demonstrating that Magnum's melodic side was apparent right from the beginning. It really takes off from around 2.04, however, with a section of frantic guitar acrobatics and darting bass before a return to the more sedate main theme. Tinkling keys bring the song to a close. It's not a standout, but 'All That is Real' is a decent track that points ahead to the more commercial offerings sprinkled across *Magnum II*.

'The Bringer' (4:58)
We're firmly back in fantasy territory with this tale of being hunted down by a malevolent creature, the eponymous 'bringer'. There's plenty of variation in the track's five minutes, moving from syncopated rhythms and verbose lyrics to a gentle chorus and then onto a weighty closing instrumental section. At the heart of the song – framed by a variety of keyboard and mellotron effects – is one of Clarkin's more immediate and striking riffs. The rhythm section holds everything together, with Gorin's insistent use of cowbell maintaining the energy and ensuring the track never drags. It may not be one of the album's most celebrated tunes, but 'The Bringer' is an enjoyable listen, providing further evidence of Magnum's early progressive tendencies.

'Invasion' (3:22)
The third part of what might be considered the Kingdom of Madness 'suite', 'Invasion' is a simple sci-fi-inspired tale of an alien attack on Earth. Lyrically, it's certainly not Clarkin's finest hour, with clunky lines such as 'Alien, your day this is not to be/All the people say "let the world be free"'. But the outlandish theme fits the frantic energy of the song perfectly. It begins with a brief multitracked Queen-style choral reprise of 'Madness', linking it both to 'In the Beginning' and the title track before moving on to a wonderful dual guitar and keyboard gallop that sets the template for the rest of the song. The whole band are on fine form throughout, but special attention should be paid to Lowe's dynamic bass line and Catley's impressive falsetto vocals.

'Invasion' was one of the more durable tunes from the debut album, continuing to be played in concert into the 1980s. It featured on both the

1980 live EP that preceded the *Marauder* album and the post-*Chase The Dragon* set when the band were supporting Ozzy Osbourne in the United States in 1982 (released in 1989 as *Invasion Live*).

'Lords Of Chaos' (3:21)

The infectious energy of side two continues with this enjoyable experiment in rock disco. A step too far perhaps for some rock fans, 'Lords Of Chaos' unashamedly embraces the disco stylings of the day with phased clavinet, funky bass and drums and loosely strummed rhythm guitar. Too much emphasis on the shuffle that drives the song forward, however, takes away from the quality of the melody in the verse and chorus. Indeed, the live version on *Marauder*, and especially Clarkin's guitar sound, is significantly heavier and fits well with the harder sound of that album. 'Lords Of Chaos' is the second Clarkin composition (after 'Stormbringer', see below) inspired by Michael Moorcock's Elric of Melniboné series of fantasy novels and short stories.

'All Come Together' (4:52)

Kingdom Of Madness ends with 'All Come Together', the third of the classic songs on the debut that confirmed the future potential of the band. Bookended by Bailey's gorgeous piano and mellotron serenade, this is a song that underlines the depth of Clarkin's compositional skill and his ability to write infectious melodies. The understated opening instrumental section and first verse give way after 53 seconds to falsetto backing vocals and an explosion of marching bass and drums. After the first chorus, the speed quickens as Bailey introduces a funky keyboard motif supported by Lowe's scurrying bass. There are a number of changes of mood and pace across the song, but the playing is tight throughout. If there's one low point, it's the slightly underwhelming middle eight at 2.20, but even this is quickly forgotten as Clarkin follows up with another inspired double-tracked guitar break.

Incorporating plenty of instrumental variety and progressive touches, 'All Come Together' is a great way to end a promising debut album. Its complexity may explain why it wasn't played live as often as some of the disc's other stand-out tracks.

Related Tracks

There are lots of additional tracks related to the early years of Magnum. The 1993 Jet compilation album *Archive*, included the 1974 Nest demos along with four tracks recorded during the 1976 *Kingdom Of Madness* sessions. The 2005 expanded two-CD reissue of *Kingdom Of Madness* featured all these tracks on the second disc with the addition of the 1975 CBS single, 'Sweets For My Sweet'/'Movin' On' (alongside the reworked 1979 version of the title track discussed above). The 2021 *Riding The Rock Machine* compilation (Grapefruit) included a further previously unreleased recording from the 1975 session, 'Baby I Need', while another previously unreleased track found by

Dave Morgan was included on 2022's *The Monster Roars* boxset. As nobody could remember the title, it was called 'Track Number Three'.

The Nest Demos
'Sea Bird' (3:49)
Clarkin's simple acoustic strumming and Gorin's dynamic percussion set the stage for a straightforward tale of lost love. This is laid-back, mellow and reminiscent of 1960s psychedelic pop. The tune is nice but unremarkable; overall, it's perhaps most notable as a lyrical precursor to *Wings Of Heaven*'s monumental 'Wild Swan'.

'Stormbringer' (3:31)
This is a funky little number making full use of Bailey's flute alongside a heavy guitar attack. Musically, it sounds rather basic and underdeveloped, but lyrically, it hints at some of the themes Clarkin was to advance a little more convincingly over the next few years. As the guitarist himself noted in 1988, the title was 'ripped off' the 1965 Michael Moorcock fantasy novel featuring the character Elric of Melniboné, also referenced in 'Lords of Chaos'. Stormbringer is the name of the magic sword that features heavily in this and many of Moorcock's other books.

'Slipping Away' (3:15)
Catley's characteristic vocal inflections are all over this likeable folk tune. With Clarkin's guitar almost buried beneath Morgan's prominent bass work and Bailey's organ, there's very little of the rock sound that was to develop on later recordings. It's an interesting indication of the direction in which Magnum might have gone if nothing else.

'Captain America' (3:43)
The rockiest of the early demos, 'Captain America' features lively Clarkin riffing and a tight rhythm track. The lyrics dwell on the comic-book exploits of Marvel characters, including Scarlet Witch, the Human Torch, Iceman and Black Panther, as well as the titular character. Some of the lines are fairly absurd, perhaps intentionally so: 'The god of thunder we all know as Thor/ Has lost his hammer and is feeling quite sore'. But it's ultimately a fairly enjoyable – if inconsequential – (almost) four minutes.

Overall, the variability of the Nest demos indicates that, as the band themselves admitted on the sleeve notes of *Archive*, they were still searching 'for a musical identity'.

1975 CBS single:
'Sweets For My Sweet' (3:03) (Doc Pomus and Mort Shuman)
The quest wasn't really helped by this energetic but ultimately fairly pointless version of The Searchers' 1963 UK number one (originally

recorded in 1961 by The Drifters). This was one of the popular hits the band were playing during their Rum Runner residency. Produced by Roger Greenaway for CBS Records because he felt it could be a hit, this version features Dave Morgan on lead vocals. It's a pretty generic, rocked-up version of a so-so track (despite its elevated chart position) with little to distinguish it. A remastered version, with the original live 'God Rest Ye Merry Gentlemen' section in the middle restored, was released as part of *The Monster Roars* box set in 2022.

'Movin' On' (3:47)

The B-side of 'Sweets for My Sweet' is one of the early tracks that signals Clarkin's ability as a writer, even if it doesn't exactly mark out the band's future direction of travel. It's a gorgeous blues rock shuffle reminiscent of the more soulful Marks III and IV incarnations of Deep Purple, with Catley doing his best Glenn Hughes impression.

The Kingdom Of Madness outtakes:
'Master Of Disguise' (2:54)

A chunky groove-based riff powers this straightforward rock workout, but it's Bailey's flute embellishments that set it apart. The wonderfully chaotic flute solo on the 1976 live version on *Days Of Wonder* is reproduced on vinyl with lovely additional flourishes floating in between the vocal lines. There are some elaborate drum fills from Gorin and Lowe's funky bass line operates neatly in unison with the guitar riff. It should and ought to have replaced 'Baby Rock Me' on the final track listing.

'Without Your Love' (3:54)

This is one of Clarkin's earliest ballads and it's not at all bad. Driven by an intricate piano refrain, one of its characteristic features is the layered gospel-style backing vocals. There's a clever false ending after which Clarkin's guitar bursts into life for the last minute. Nonetheless, the subtler, pared-down live version, as heard on *Days Of Wonder*, is superior.

'Find The Time' (3:04)

It's not entirely surprising that 'Find The Time' was one of the early recordings dropped from the final album. One of the least memorable of the 1976 session tracks, it has an airy, buoyant mood that doesn't entirely fit with the majority of the material on the record. The unexpected chord sequence in the middle eight is the best part of the song.

'Everybody Needs' (3:47)

Another fairly standard rock tune with hints of Queen, 'Everybody Needs' is lifted by a bluesy Clarkin solo and a powerful Catley vocal performance, augmented by one of Magnum's most successful early experiments with harmonised backing vocals. The band obviously rated the song as it was re-recorded in 1980 as a B-Side to the remixed 'Changes' single. That version, produced by Leo Lyons with additional production by Chris Tsangarides, is almost a minute shorter and has punchier guitars and a more stompy, fist-pumping chorus.

Other Tracks
'Baby I Need' (2:57) (Dave Morgan)
A rare Magnum recording not written by Tony Clarkin, 'Baby I Need' unsurprisingly sounds like nothing else in the band's catalogue. It's an interesting slice of early 1970s power pop, reminiscent of Alex Chilton's Big Star. The *Riding The Rock Machine* liner notes claim Bob Catley to be the vocalist, but it sounds like it could be Morgan. It's dated 1975 and was apparently recorded at Nest Studios at the same time as another Morgan composition, 'One More Round The Bend', which was sung by Catley.

'Track Number Three' (4:28)
Found among Dave Morgan's old tapes of the band, this is a fairly unassuming sixties-style pop tune. What sets it apart, and possibly connects it to later Clarkin compositions, is the inclusion of discrete sections and changing time signatures. It opens with the main riff from 'Slipping Away' but then develops in a completely different direction. Based on a rapid strummed rhythm guitar and a catchy guitar run, the first section is the best part of the song. The second, slower section, reminiscent of Bowie, and the chorus, with its 'But it's all passed me by/That's all I can hear' refrain, are rather more generic and conventional.

Magnum II (1979)

Personnel:
Tony Clarkin: guitar and vocals
Bob Catley: lead vocal
Richard Bailey: keyboards, vocals and flute
Colin 'Wally' Lowe: bass guitar and vocals
Kex Gorin: drums and percussion
Produced at De Lane Lea Studios/Music Centre Studios, Wembley, London by
Leo Lyons
Engineer: Rafe McKenna
Assistant Engineer: Paul Hume
Release date: 19 October 1979 on Jet Records
Cover Design: Original design uncredited; re-released 1998 album illustration,
Rodney Matthews
Highest chart places: UK, West Germany and Sweden: Did not chart
Running time: 40:33

In the summer of 1979, less than a year after the release of their debut
album, Magnum convened at De Lane Lea (also known as Music Centre)
Studios in London to record the follow-up. Much of the material that
constituted what became *Magnum II* had been written over the previous
couple of years and road-tested alongside the *Kingdom Of Madness* songs.
While elements of the complex, progressive arrangements that characterised
the debut remained, overall, the songs were more direct and concise. As
Richard Bailey remarked in a 2022 interview: 'We employed quite a different
approach on that one; we wanted to sound more polished and a bit less
raw, like the big American rock bands'.

Former Ten Years After bassist Leo Lyons was hired to refine the Magnum
sound. He was an established producer, having become studio manager
at Chrysalis Records' Wessex Studios in 1975 and producing a trio of UFO
albums – *Phenomenon* (1974), *Force It* (1975) and *No Heavy Petting* (1976)
– that helped define that band as an influential hard rock act. Jet's David
Arden apparently chose Lyons, but Clarkin and Co. seem to have approved
of the decision and certainly got on well with him.

Magnum II was the album where Bailey really came into his own in
helping to shape the group's sound. Although it was more refined, Lyons
still allowed space for sonic experimentation and there was particular room
for the elaborate flourishes of Bailey's keyboards. Press reports at the time
tended to focus on Clarkin and Bailey as the key members of Magnum. As
one report in the *Burton Daily Mail* put it, while Clarkin may have been the
'creator', the classically-influenced multi-instrumentalist 'also had a major
effect' on 'Magnum's sound'. Clarkin himself observed that the keyboards
dominated the arrangements, with the rest of the group playing along to
them in the studio.

In contrast to the debut's positive reception, however, the music press generally panned *Magnum II*. In *Sounds*, Geoff Barton gave the album three stars and complained that the more professional recording had also resulted in 'a bland-out American sound which doesn't suit Magnum at all'. Malcolm Dome in the *Record Mirror* considered the album 'a disappointment' and 'a dumbed-down diluted version of their debut, from the title onwards'. He complained that it seemed as if:

> Some bright spark at Jet decided to take them out of the *Kingdom Of Madness* into a high-quality nursing home, inject Tony Clarkin with vinyl solutions of Foreigner and Journey and install trustworthy head 'nurse', Leo Lyons … to convince the band that they too could find success in the AOR market.

At the time, Clarkin largely defended the production but accepted that the keyboards may have been a little mechanical and later recalled that the drum sound was 'really flat'.

For all of the criticism it received at the time, *Magnum II* represents a clear improvement both in the overall quality of the songs and the performances. The material on the album is nowhere near as one-dimensional as Barton and Dome's reviews suggest. Indeed, in retrospect, *Magnum II* might be considered to have successfully fine-tuned the varied collage of sounds present on *Kingdom Of Madness*. The album retains fantasy-based epic songs, such as 'Great Adventure', 'Reborn' and 'Firebird', though these are more concise than on the debut. But it adds to this a couple of lavish anthems ('If I Could Live Forever' and 'All Of My Life') as well as the more straight-ahead attempts to move into commercial territory, with 'Changes' and 'Foolish Heart'. Overall, *Magnum II* is an overlooked record, with a more consistent range of material than both the album that preceded it and the one that followed.

The no-nonsense black text on the silver sleeve reflects the simpler approach the band were going for, but it doesn't do the album any favours. Press adverts added a ladle pouring hot metal onto the sleeve's Roman numerals, presumably in an attempt to link the band to some sort of masculine hard rock imagery. As with *Kingdom Of Madness*, FM Records' 1998 reissue planted the record in a sleeve with a seemingly random Rodney Matthews illustration, his pre-existing sci-fi inspired 'To Steal A Battleship'.

'Great Adventure' (4:54)
The album opens with this brilliantly atmospheric tour-de-force. It's like a tougher and leaner 'In the Beginning', with a similar combination of progressive twists and turns packed into a more palatable five minutes.

A howling wolf and wind effects set the aural scene of a desolate landscape, with Bailey's synth mimicking the sound of a galloping horse and giving the impression of a quest in progress. Underneath all this, Bailey's keyboards announce a slowed-down version of the main theme. At around 40 seconds, the introduction fades, a pulsating bass synth comes to the fore and Catley's near-whispered vocal arrives, accompanied by punchy guitar and drums and multi-tracked backing vocals. Bailey's rich synth motif raises the bar further still and the song takes off from here.

The second verse brings in a higher, impassioned Catley vocal with some lovely interplay between acoustic and electric guitar ushering in a delightful, melodic chorus. Clarkin launches into a heavy instrumental break between 2.15 and 2.45, with clever use of double-tracked guitar lines and Lowe's bass dancing along underneath and then we're back to the main theme but with added crunch. A Gorin drum fill leads into the final minute and the song seems to be petering out with light keyboard and acoustic guitar before some soloing from Clarkin speeds things up and the track then ends abruptly with a cymbal crash.

Clarkin remembers writing the song while on a family holiday in a caravan in the coastal resort of Weymouth in southern England – an image that contrasts with the rather generalised fantasy tale of 'a journey far beyond my dreams' involving 'a silver sea' and 'forbidden treasure'. 'It was Weymouth that brought that song out of me', Clarkin told Dave Ling in the 2005 expanded edition sleeve notes, 'daydreaming of some big adventure'.

Whatever the meaning, 'Great Adventure' is one of Magnum's finest early tracks; a successful fusion of intricate musicianship, raw power and melody. A reasonable live version appeared on the 1980 Live EP, but thereafter, it disappeared from the set, possibly because it didn't reflect the more direct approach the band were then signalling.

'Changes' (3:15)

The first single from *Magnum II*, released in September 1979 (with 'Lonesome Star' on the B-side), was, by Clarkin's own admission, him 'trying to be commercial'. It may not have worked in terms of record sales, but it did demonstrate another important string to the guitarist's songwriting bow, which he was to build on so effectively from the mid-1980s. Bailey's keyboard textures are again prominent, even if the piano embellishments towards the end are a little predictable. But Clarkin and Catley are the real stars of this track; the former executing one of his most simple but effective riffs, while the latter nails the vocal, at the same time flagging up his quality as a more than adequate AOR vocalist.

On the back of the success of *Marauder* – which featured a confident rendition of the song – Jet decided to release a remixed version of the 'Changes' single in June 1980, with enhanced backing vocals and a more delicate keyboard sound. However, it fared no better in the charts.

'The Battle' (2:10)

Like 'Changes', 'The Battle' had been written prior to the release of *Kingdom Of Madness* but was held over for the second album. As such, it's not surprising that it shared a similar fantasy approach found on the debut, with conflict and war already emerging as one of Clarkin's core lyrical preoccupations. As one of the shortest songs in the band's catalogue, it's also one of the most intense – a concentrated swirl of progressive synths, chunky guitar riffs and a super tight rhythm section but with space for a fantastic keyboard solo with more than a passing nod to the then-embryonic British neo-prog sound.

The version of the song the band were playing live in 1976 (included on the retrospective live collection *Days Of Wonder*) was around a minute and a half longer. It incorporated a meandering funky guitar opening and a variation on the chorus, with a more radical reduction of tempo and a near instrumental drop-out for the lines, 'Now there will be no morning'.

'If I Could Live Forever' (4:02)
This was one of Clarkin's first attempts to create a genuine pomp anthem, mixing musical virtuosity and structural complexity with a plethora of melodic hooks. In the 2005 edition sleeve notes, the guitarist remembered that he had wanted 'to make a really dramatic statement' with the song and that when it was played live, the intention was 'to have lots of light and shade. It had to be grandiose'.

It opens in lavish style with sombre piano chords and synths backed by a huge mellotron choir. 'Friday night is almost over', Catley croons over shimmering keys and then a massive guitar chord brings in the rest of the band. We're then straight into a bouncy two-part chorus that moves the song firmly into AOR territory. At 2.10, the verse switches to double-time accompanied by harmonised twin guitar parts and Clarkin delivers a brilliant solo over more duelling guitars as the song moves towards its fade out.

Overall, it's a cleverly constructed tune, with Catley's overwrought vocals a particular highlight. But the *Magnum II* studio version pales next to its live *Marauder* counterpart, which delivers substantially more power and a guitar tone that's much heavier.

'Reborn' (5:45)
Next up is another multi-part piece that provides more evidence of the band's ability to successfully mix up soaring tunes with progressive structures. Opening with a bluesy guitar and piano groove, it soon settles into a joyful rock track with an edge, characterised by frequent shifts between sections and tempo changes. A serene acoustic guitar and flute interlude after the first chorus reinforces the band's folk tendencies, as had been evident in 'Kingdom of Madness', and there are some lovely instrumental sections with Bailey's piano and Lowe's freewheeling bass, particularly to the fore. Variations on the main themes and riffs tumble over one another in the final minute, as the vocals return, but somehow everything holds together perfectly.

'Reborn' manages to hold its progressive and melodic rock elements in balance effectively over its nearly six-minute duration. Be sure to check out the *Marauder* version of this one too, which rocks and swings in equal measure and sounds amazing.

'So Cold The Night' (4:04)
Side two of the original vinyl begins with this moody track, which includes one of the heaviest riffs in the Magnum catalogue. Accompanied by martial drums and an almost doomy guitar refrain, this is a powerful opening and probably the closest the band ever got to sounding like fellow Birmingham rockers Black Sabbath. On first listen, the cheery keyboard riff that arrives at 42 seconds seems ill-suited to both the mood and metre of the track, but ultimately, the contrast seems to work. It's also another *Magnum II* song that demonstrates Catley's growing confidence as a vocalist.

'Foolish Heart' (3:13)
The second single from the album, released in November 1979 with 'Baby Rock Me' on the reverse, is another attempt at fairly mainstream AOR. The 'lighter stuff' was, as Clarkin noted in 2005, meant to 'break up the record. It improves the flow and makes it more complete'. 'I always think it's a mistake to make an album that's serious from start to finish', he added. 'Foolish Heart' does that job ably and it's a pretty solid straight-ahead rocker with some great stabbed piano chords and swirling synths, a warm undulating bass groove and more Thin Lizzy-esque twin guitar. Clarkin was also clearly learning to package his more commercial material with simpler lyrical themes, as with this unfussy narrative of a broken relationship. It's not up to the standard of 'Changes' but, as with a number of the less involved tracks on the album, it packed a significantly harder punch live and on the *Marauder* record. This single also failed to chart.

'Stayin' Alive' (3:22)
This isn't a bad track, but given the overall consistency of the record, it is perhaps the weakest link in the chain. The album's ballad contains the type of pinpoint emotive Catley vocal that was to become a feature of the next decade or so. Acoustic guitar, piano and mellotron choir also combine to great effect, with the main let-down being the rather syrupy soft rock finale in the chorus and the song as a whole. With two stronger AOR numbers from *Magnum II* in the set, it's reasonable that 'Stayin' Alive' wasn't played much live. A bold move, though, to use the exact same title as a recent mega disco hit from one of the most popular movie soundtracks of the 1970s that had reached number one in eight countries.

'Firebird' (4:47)
The third and final of the album's prog mini-epics (or mini-prog epics), 'Firebird' is a fairly complex stop-start composition with a foot in folk-rock as well as prog. While the interchange between guitar, keyboard and

drums (complete with mellotron choir at the beginning) is possibly as close as Magnum came to actually sounding like Yes, there are also a number of Jethro Tull-like passages. Indeed, the short medieval jig between 2.12-2.25, complete with flute and harpsichord, is close to parody. At the core of the track, however, is a fairly straightforward rock tune, underpinned by crunching guitar and tight hard rock harmonies. If it's the least accessible of the proggier tracks, it still demonstrates Clarkin's ability to work up a range of disparate musical ideas into a coherent whole and an enjoyable listening experience.

'All Of My Life' (4:43)
The finale of *Magnum II* is this fabulous juggernaut that builds from a basic musical idea into an elaborate rock anthem. Quizzed about it in 2005, Clarkin recalled that it was one of the tracks in which he 'wanted to incorporate a few extra time changes, just to see if they'd work'. He did note that being 'really clever' in this way didn't always work if 'it's not very good on the ears', although it's not clear whether or not he was referring to this song in particular.

A walking bass line and jazzy piano usher in one of the band's more direct melodies and a great singalong chorus that forms the spine of the song. From that point, it's about building momentum and variations on the main theme, with the tension increasing as the musicians, especially Gorin on drums, are allowed to let rip. The melodic bridge adds a little diversity and from Catley's Robert Plant-inspired 'Yeah' at 2.19, there's a sped-up version of the chorus before a second bridge and a dramatic stage ending.

Touching on themes of war and loss, 'All Of My Life' had been a key element of the band's set since 1976. It continued to offer an opportunity for the musicians to stretch out on stage for another couple of tours, although some of the less successful experiments (such as the jarring synth sounds as heard on *Days Of Wonder*) were sensibly cut from the studio version.

Related Tracks
'Lonesome Star' (3:13)
The B-side to 'Changes' is a pleasant enough but fairly undistinguished, mid-paced, keyboard-heavy, melodic rocker. The lyrics seem to be broadly situated in Clarkin's fantasy realm and the most significant feature of the song is probably the last appearance of Bailey's flute in the instrumental break.

Chase The Dragon (1982)

Personnel:
Tony Clarkin: guitars, acoustic guitars and vocals
Bob Catley: lead vocals
Mark Stanway: keyboards
Wally Lowe: bass guitar and vocals
Kex Gorin: drums
Produced and engineered at Townhouse Studios, London by Jeff Glixman
Assistant engineer: Steve Presage
Release date: 24 February 1982 on Jet Records
Cover Design: Rodney Matthews
Highest chart places: UK: 17, West Germany and Sweden: Did not chart
Running time: 35:19

Although *Magnum II* had failed to chart, the band remained an attractive
live proposition, touring with Blue Öyster Cult in November 1979 in the UK
and with UFO in December in mainland Europe. Jet's decision to record one
of the band's concerts at the Marquee Club in London in November 1979
transformed their fortunes. The resulting record, *Marauder* – released in
April 1980 and featuring two tracks from *Kingdom Of Madness* and six from
Magnum II – was the band's first to chart, reaching a respectable number 34
in the UK. It was preceded by a four-track 'Live EP' (released March 1980)
that, equally impressively, made it to number 47 in the singles chart. Clarkin
has since said that he felt Jet Records would have ditched the band had
Marauder 'not taken off the way it did'.

By this point, Richard Bailey had left the band, disappointed by the lack
of success and struggling with the clichéd musical differences. As he noted
in a *Fireworks* interview in 2022: 'While the others liked it heavy, I was
more into bands like Steely Dan. So I decided to move on'. He was briefly
replaced by Grenville Harding, who played during a tour with Def Leppard
in April 1980, but personality clashes led to the band firing him within a
few weeks.

Ultimately, Magnum recruited Mark Stanway (born in 1954), a keyboardist
with Birmingham jazz-rock bands Rainmaker and Little Acre. He passed a
bizarre audition playing the tricky synth riff from 'Invasion' while members
of the band and crew were drunkenly doing acrobatics and letting off
pyrotechnics.

Chase The Dragon was recorded in June 1980 at Townhouse in west
London, a state-of-the-art studio set up by Virgin boss Richard Branson
just two years earlier. It was produced by Jeff Glixman, who had been
responsible for twiddling the knobs on four albums by American
progressive rock band Kansas including *Leftoverture* (1976) and *Point
Of Know Return* (1977). Clarkin recalled in the liner notes to the 2005
expanded edition being delighted at the appointment: 'The combination of

a super producer like Jeff and a great studio like Townhouse was something we could only have dreamed of'.

The writing and recording of *Chase The Dragon* was much quicker than earlier records. The band rehearsed for only a fortnight and recorded the basic tracks in four days, with the rest of the work completed in a little over a week more. Previously, songs had been played live for a year or so before recording, but on this occasion, the band learnt the songs and immediately recorded them, often in a single take. Clarkin would write on an acoustic guitar through the night and bring songs he'd finished to rehearsals the following day. 'The beauty' of this way of doing things, Clarkin noted in a May 1982 *Kerrang!* interview, 'was that the music seemed so fresh to us'. Clarkin also remembered being very happy with the material he'd written for the record. 'There were none of the hang-ups I had with previous albums', he observed in the 2005 liner notes, 'I was extremely confident'.

However, serious financial problems at Jet Records led to a substantial delay in the final mixing and release of the album. It seems that on top of the general economic tensions of the period, the label was being pressured by one of their leading acts, ELO, to unpick the chaotic finances associated with that band. As a result, Jet tightened the purse strings to such a degree that they were unable to pay the studio bill due to Townhouse, which in turn meant that the studio refused to release the master tapes. Clarkin remembers the frustration of constantly phoning up the label (the band didn't have an independent manager at this time) to see if things had been resolved. Finally, at some point in late 1981/early 1982, Jet paid the bill, the tapes were released and Clarkin was able to travel to Glixman's Axis Studios in Atlanta to do a few guitar overdubs and oversee the final mix of the album.

Chase The Dragon was the first Magnum album to feature the artwork of renowned fantasy artist Rodney Matthews. Matthews had contacted Clarkin after reading an interview with the guitarist. He had already produced sleeves for NWOBHM bands, Praying Mantis and Tygers of Pan Tang, and illustrated Michael Moorcock books – therefore, he seemed a logical fit. Matthews produced two paintings for the album, with the original title of *The Spirit*. The idea was that the two images would form a gatefold sleeve. The one eventually used on the cover, of an eastern-looking city in the distance with a dragon and a tree at the forefront, would be viewed together with a painting called 'Sanctuary', depicting the same city millions of years in the future. The intention, as Matthews revealed in a 2017 *Rock Candy* interview, was that 'the city might have aged over millions of years, but the spirit it represents is untouched'.

Clarkin changed the name of the album at the last minute after hearing the phrase 'Chase the Dragon' (referring to smoking heroin) from a roadie and deciding it was a great title. The connection to Matthews' concept was lost, although luckily, the cover image did feature a dragon. Jet also abandoned the idea of a gatefold sleeve due to the costs involved. Matthews also created the band's first (and most enduring) logo on the sleeve, incorporating Moorcock's 'Sword Of Chaos' into the lettering for the 'M'.

With the album's release in February 1982, the fortunes of the band took a sharp upturn. Despite not garnering outstanding reviews – Chris Welch in *Kerrang!* viewed it as a 'pleasant, varied but surprisingly conservative set of performances' – *Chase The Dragon* was the first Magnum record to breach the UK Top 20, peaking at number seventeen. After supporting Swiss band Krokus in February 1982, they undertook a headlining 'Sword of Chaos' UK tour in March. In the spring, Magnum supported label mate Ozzy Osbourne on the second leg of his *Diary Of A Madman* US arena tour, which included the recordings at Nashville Municipal Auditorium that made it onto the October 1982 'Live In America' EP and 1989's *Invasion Live* album.

Chase The Dragon was a step forward in sound and performance. Clarkin certainly felt the band were technically better players by this point and Gilxman's production was sharper than on previous Magnum albums. The album's popularity at the time may have partly been because it incorporated a more straightforward sound closer to some of the heavy rock bands Magnum were touring with. The complexity and intricacy remained, especially in the three standout tracks, 'Soldier Of The Line', 'The Spirit' and 'Sacred Hour'. Yet the more direct approach also downplayed some of the quirky originality that had characterised the first two albums and set Magnum apart from the pack.

'Soldier Of The Line' (4:16)

A career-defining track, 'Soldier Of The Line' is powerful, heavy and to the point. A reflection on the psychology of conflict from the soldier's perspective, it dwells on themes that Clarkin would return to a number of times in his songwriting career. For example, battlefield experiences and the spectre of early death are taken up in 'Don't Wake The Lion' and 'Dance Of The Black Tattoo', while the notion of the unremembered/nameless dead, alluded to in the final lines, recurs in later songs such as 'No One Knows His Name' and 'Unwritten Sacrifice'. With its references to combatants being stuck in a 'murderous playground', the lyrics seem to be a timeless comment on what Clarkin called 'the foolishness of war', although mentions of 'castle walls', 'armour' and 'flag and lance' depicts a medieval/pre-modern rather than a modern landscape.

The moody introduction seems to mimic the clanking of armour and weapons and the series of loud bangs were meant, according to Stanway's autobiography, to resemble thunder. The latter sound came from the keyboardist throwing the lid of his electric grand piano onto the floor as hard as possible; this was then slowed down and echo was added. At 49 seconds, the music arrives with a series of power chords, simple one-note keyboard accompaniment and Clarkin's vocal. It's incredibly effective, as the layering builds with a repeating synth riff, drums and then, finally (on 1.53), a pulsating Lowe bass line joining the ensemble. Then we're onto the pre-chorus, the brilliant chorus (surely one of Clarkin's very best melodies) and a harmonised guitar and keyboard refrain. In the second verse, background group and main vocals swap places in an effective call-and-response and the momentum of the track builds as the pace quickens to an abrupt finish.

It's a great song, musically and lyrically heavy, with as much appeal to metal fans as to 1970s hard rockers.

'On The Edge Of The World' (4:22)

At one point proposed as the title track, 'On The Edge Of The World' represents a pared down, no-frills Magnum and is the most successful of the elementary rock tunes on the album. Beginning with spacey synth effects, it then moves at around 45 seconds to a pretty conventional melodic rock tune. Some of the nicest touches include the brief Thin Lizzy-style twin guitar breaks and Stanway's occasional mini-Moog interventions. Overall, it's a fairly raw production but powerful nonetheless, with Catley's vocals particularly standing out.

'The Spirit' (4:17)

Encapsulating the band's fondness for combining progressive, folk and hard rock styles, 'The Spirit' is at the same time one of Magnum's most ornate and one of their most direct songs. Instrumentally, it's a lavish production, moving from picked acoustic to heavy guitars through intricate harpsichord accompaniment, then a heavy rock interlude incorporating scurrying bass, crashing drums and one of Clarkin's more expressive solos. Structurally, however, it's a pretty simple affair: a repeated verse with a slight variation in the chorus and one change in tack for the short middle eight. As with a number of the songs on *Chase The Dragon*, 'The Spirit' works by building from relatively sparse beginnings to a heavier, intensified full-band performance.

While written vaguely enough to be interpreted in a number of ways, the lyrics certainly align with Clarkin's Christian beliefs. It's a song about hope and believing (whether in a particular faith or oneself) but also warns of the dangers that can send you on the wrong path, such as 'foolish promises', 'shallow verse' and 'street corner justice'. There's a complexity in the language and a depth to the writing that set the band apart from most other popular hard rock acts of the early 1980s. But its profundity didn't stop the song from making an immediate impact and becoming one of the *Chase The Dragon* tracks that stuck in the setlist for over a decade. It was also a track that the band experimented with considerably on stage, often by introducing longer acoustic sections.

'The Spirit' is one of the few Magnum songs to have been covered by another artist. The German heavy metal band Edguy, led by Tobias Sammet, who was to become part of the Magnum story later, recorded a fairly faithful version in 2005 as part of their 'Superheroes' EP.

'Sacred Hour' (5:35)

This is one of the undisputed pearls in the Magnum catalogue. Indulgent, grandiose and ostentatious, it reflects some of the band's earlier progressive and so-called 'pomp' rock influences but it's also a deeply moving piece of music that encapsulates the emotion of Clarkin's writing and Catley's singing.

It begins with a majestic piano and organ melody that was apparently adapted by Stanway from a piece that had been written by his wife, Mo Birch. This introduction was certainly not included in early live performances – such as the Reading Festival show in 1980 – or on the early demo. At 1.10, this stops and the original theme returns on the piano. Catley's beautiful vocal floats over the top and then at 2.00, there's a drum roll, but it's another half minute before the whole band enter with guitar, stabbed keyboard chords and a muscular Lowe bass line. Stanway's role is central throughout as he introduces a number of synth phrases and effects to add to the strident energy of the track. It ends in true theatrical style with an extended stage ending.

As well as a tremendous piece of music, 'Sacred Hour' may be one of Clarkin's best lyrics. It's a serious attempt to reflect upon the experience of the live concert from the point of view of the performer. Moving from a fairly conventional depiction of the concert as an 'hour' out of time, in which the troubles and concerns of everyday life 'take second place', the narrative cleverly captures the fragility of the live communion and the performers' anxieties at the nature of the relationship with the audience:

I can hear them calling
I can hear the crowd applauding
If it's real I like the feeling
If I'm wrong, who am I deceiving?

Some of the lines provide as succinct a picture of the gig experience as in any rock song: 'Night after night/It repeats an exciting romance/Shared by us all/Though we meet by a fleeting half chance'. As Michael Anthony put it in his 2012 book *Words And Music*, 'Sacred Hour' encapsulated 'the joy, the wonder and the fragility of the live gig experience in a five-and-a-half minute nutshell'.

In relation to the title, it's interesting that Clarkin has noted a number of times that some commentators have mistakenly attached a direct Christian message to the song. Nonetheless, the choice of the word 'sacred' is revealing, and it's a term the guitarist was to use frequently in his subsequent writing.

Hardcore fans might be interested to know that 'Sacred Hour' has been sampled on no fewer than three rap tracks, including sped-up versions on Philadelphian hip-hop artist Reef the Lost Cauze's 2010 *Fight Music* album and American-Venezuelan rapper Emilio Rojas' '585 (Roc Y'all Remix)' in 2009.

'Walking The Straight Line' (4:53)

Side two of the vinyl starts with this decent but fairly uninspired hard rock track. The playing is great, as is the production. Clarkin's guitar break at 2.38 displays a new-found confidence in taking centre stage when needed. The rhythm section also sounds really tight here, with Lowe's sliding and walking bass lines especially prominent. But it's ultimately a fairly predictable song with Stanway's keyboards kept at the margins and very few surprises. The arrangement on the 1980 demo version, with a bit more of a boogie feel and additional piano fills, might have worked better on the final recording.

'We All Play The Game' (4:07)

Things improve markedly with this flowing partial ballad, one of the tracks that sounds closest to the band's first two albums. Led by Stanway's haunting mini-Moog phrase on top of strummed acoustic guitar, this is also reminiscent of the opening of Yes' classic, 'And You And I' from *Close To The Edge*. But while that track drifted atmospherically, this one moves with a little more pace and urgency. It builds to a serviceable chorus, but the song is at its best in the warm chord changes, vocal harmonies and keyboard embellishments of the verses. Special note should also be made of Lowe's rich, chunky bass line, one of a number of fine bass performances on the album.

'The Teacher' (3:21)

Clarkin is the star of this blues rock workout. It's a pretty simple song, driven along by a meaty Deep Purple-inspired guitar riff over which Catley lays down an ardent vocal with a vague fantasy theme. The most exciting part is the instrumental section in the middle where, after a brief jazzy piano break, Stanway launches into an urgent keyboard riff which is underpinned by harmonised guitar and ferocious drumming. Clarkin embarks on another frantic guitar solo – and some head-down jamming – in the last minute of the song and we're done. Once again, the album version is more guitar-heavy than the demo, which included piano tinkling in the background during the verses and Clarkin and Stanway indulging in trade-off solos towards the end. It's not surprising that the song was streamlined to sound a little heavier and more contemporary but it rendered it more generic than it might have been as a result.

'The Lights Burned Out' (4:32)

The finale to the album is this popular yet rather saccharine piano ballad. Catley's vocal takes the lead role here and it's undoubtedly a fine performance. The chorus is beefy and reasonably memorable, too, while Clarkin delivers a bluesy solo with genuine feeling. Yet, while the sentimentality of the music befits a tale of lost love, it doesn't quite have the depth or the melodic strength of some of Magnum's later ballads. It certainly became a popular live track and band members enjoyed playing it, but it's always seemed a little over-rated to me.

The original version, which was included on 1993's *Archive* and on the 2005 extended edition of the album, was recorded at Zella Studios, Birmingham, in late 1979. It has a different piano introduction and an impressive soulful Catley vocal. There's a guitar solo in place of the chorus, which had not yet been written. The 1980 demo has the chorus but is more laid back than the final take, with jazzy piano at the beginning.

'The Lights Burned Out' (b/w 'Long Days, Black Nights') was the only single taken from the album. The single version was edited down to 3.40, cutting out the second and third stanzas of the first verse. It came resplendent in a pink rendering of the album cover and with a special offer for a free 'Sword of Chaos' pendant. Despite this, it didn't chart.

Related Tracks
'Long Days, Black Nights' (3:10)
For the B-side of 'The Lights Burned Out', the record company encouraged the band to release a left-over track still in demo form. Nonetheless, this isn't at all bad. It's a dynamic hard rock composition buoyed by a chugging guitar riff, stabbed keyboard chords and some intricate guitar and keyboard back-and-forth in the instrumental break. Its pomp rock feel – not unlike Styx – may have been why it wasn't considered for inclusion on the album.

The Eleventh Hour (1983)

Personnel:
Tony Clarkin: guitar and vocals
Bob Catley: lead vocals
Mark Stanway: keyboards
Wally Lowe: bass guitar and vocals
Kex Gorin: drums and percussion
Produced at Portland Studios, London by Tony Clarkin, assisted by Bob Catley
Engineer: Dave Garland
Release date: 13 May 1983 on Jet Records
Cover Design: Rodney Matthews
Highest chart places: UK: 38, West Germany and Sweden: Did not chart
Running time: 39:38

With a stockpile of material gathered due to the delay of *Chase The Dragon*, Magnum's fourth studio album wasn't long in coming. Clarkin was keen for Jeff Glixman to produce again, but the record company, eager to economise, suggested the band do the job themselves. 'I remember', Clarkin noted in the sleeve notes to the 2005 expanded edition, 'David Arden [of Jet] saying, "It's about time you started producing yourselves". I just went "Gulp!", but it forced my hand'.

The band seemed to have begun recording early in 1982. Stanway noted in his autobiography that they had started work on the new album at Jet's studio in Portland Place before flying over to the US to support Ozzy Osbourne in April 1982. The *Archive* compilation also notes that one of the outtakes intended for *The Eleventh Hour* that ended up on the expanded edition, 'True Fine Love', was recorded at Portland Studios 'in early 1982'. The two new songs that appeared as part of the 'Live In America' EP in November 1982 – 'Back To Earth' and 'Hold Back Your Love' – were also recorded at Portland in 1982 and hence are dealt with as 'related tracks' to this album rather than its predecessor.

Clarkin's experiences producing the album were mixed. He'd absorbed plenty of ideas from watching Glixman in particular and admitted to being excited about putting into practice what he'd learnt. The band also benefitted from not being under too much time pressure as the studio belonged to their record company. However, the pressure of doing two jobs eventually affected Clarkin. As he told Malcolm Dome in *Kerrang!* in May 1983:

I found producing and playing on the same album a horrible experience. I'd much prefer to have the onus on one without the other. There's so much responsibility on your shoulders when you're the musician and producer.

The consensus now seems to be that the album was badly produced, but not everyone saw it that way at the time. In his *Kerrang!* review, Mark Putterford praised Clarkin's production for affording the material 'a rough kind of edge

... which saves the songs from slipping into the ultra-slick sound which ... spoils bands like Styx'. Putterford felt that, as a result, the record has 'a more *British* feel'. Clarkin himself thought it came out 'rather well' at the time but, by 1988, had changed his mind, admitting to *Metal Hammer* that while the songs had been 'great, very adventurous', it 'sounded like a pile of s**t' and that the studio 'was like the BBC in 1930'. Others have complained about the muddy production and in his May 1983 interview with the band, Malcolm Dome argued that there were insufficient overdubs and none of the 'intricate harmonic balances' that had characterised Glixman's job on the previous album.

The sound isn't as bright as *Chase The Dragon*, certainly, but this is more than made up for by the quality and coherence of the material. *The Eleventh Hour* is in many ways a more obvious successor to *Magnum II* in that it cleverly synthesises folk, progressive and heavy rock influences into intricate but incredibly catchy three and four-minute songs. It's a sophisticated record with less obvious mainstream appeal than *Chase The Dragon*; not surprising, in view of the fact that Clarkin and Catley had apparently agreed (perhaps jokingly) they wanted to make 'a really uncommercial album'. Clarkin considered it at the time as 'a more extreme LP than *Chase The Dragon*, in that it has more obviously in-depth passages and then, by way of contrast, sudden changes into lighter passages'. It was also heavily marked by Stanway's keyboard playing. The band later interpreted the album's complexity in a negative light, but it might alternatively be considered the artistic culmination of the first phase of Magnum's career.

The cover art, again by Rodney Matthews, is among the most striking produced for the band. The idea for the figure on the throne (wearing a mask to hide his true identity and intentions), the listening children (referencing the track 'Young And Precious Souls') and the industrial wasteland came from Clarkin. Matthews added the flying aircraft in formation (arranged like ducks on the wall of a domestic house) and the shark missiles popping out from silos. The album title was, in part, a not-so-subtle dig at Jet Records' propensity to leave everything until the last minute, but there's a deeper message reflecting Clarkin's concern with the fate of civilisation depicted in what Matthews described in his 1997 *Countdown To Millennium* book as 'a sort of "Last Days" scenario'. In his appreciation of the album in *Words And Pictures*, Michael Anthony noted the historical backdrop of the rise of materialism, Cold War tensions and fear of nuclear war against which the album was conceived and provided many of its themes, which Matthews' cover art reflected and reinforced. The cover featured a different Magnum logo with gleaming gold at the top of the lettering and cracking earth at the bottom, in line with the cover image.

The Eleventh Hour wasn't as successful as the band or label had hoped for, reaching number 38 in the UK album charts. For the UK tour, a second guitarist, Robin George, was added to the line-up temporarily to help Clarkin reproduce the complex guitar parts on the record. There was talk of another US tour, but Jet's limited support for the band waned further when the album failed to match its predecessor's chart success. Around their second Reading Festival performance in August 1983 and a concert at Birmingham's Tower Ballroom in September, there were rumours that these would be Magnum's last gigs. Catley even contacted journalist Malcolm Dome to ask if he knew of any band that needed a vocalist.

The low ebb the band found themselves in towards the end of 1983 shouldn't, however, deflect from the quality and consistency of what is perhaps the most underrated of all Magnum albums.

'The Prize' (3:39)

'The Prize' is one of Clarkin's very best compositions, perfectly melding folky textures and hard rock power. It opens with a medley of acoustic guitar picking, which, like much of the album, is involved yet tuneful. Catley's urgent vocal gets things underway and then the rest of the band crash in. The riff dominates at first, but it's the strident bass line (a feature of the whole album) and chugging rhythm guitar that provide the forward motion. Spacey synth effects segue into the 'No more winners or losers' chorus and Clarkin delivers a few sparkling guitar licks before the verse and chorus repeat.

Clarkin's acoustic playing is a feature of this song and much of the album. He apparently achieved the 12-string sound by double-tracking two six-string guitars with slightly different tunings. Stanway also notes in his autobiography that Clarkin recorded in the toilet of the studio as it had the appropriate sound quality to achieve the echo slap back on 'The Prize'.

'The Prize' was one of four songs chosen for a BBC Radio One Friday Rock Show session that was recorded on the day of the album's official release and first transmitted on 27 May. Robin George, on rhythm guitar, was added to the band for this session. The recordings, produced by the BBC's Tony Wilson, are reasonable but tend to flatten the dynamics of the original and bring the guitars to the fore at the expense of the keyboards.

'Breakdown' (3:59)

A heavy groove underpins a song that deals with life's obstacles and setbacks and the fragility of the human condition. The lyrics in the chorus – 'You start to breakdown, breakdown/You're going to crucify yourself, you're lost' – are particularly intense and delivered appropriately with significant angst by Catley. In the *Vigilante* tour programme, Clarkin mentioned the song as one of the most meaningful to him.

It's a slow and steady track propelled by a muscular bass and drum arrangement. Stanway orchestrates proceedings with an array of keyboard and synth sounds, most notably medieval-style strings courtesy of the Emulator sampler hired for the sessions. Clarkin, by contrast, stays in the background save for a soulful guitar solo towards the end. Musically and lyrically downbeat it may be, but, like most of the album, it's classy and, most importantly, full of hooks. The Friday Rock Show rendition is more guitar-oriented but otherwise fairly similar to the album version.

'The Great Disaster' (3:46)
The tempo changes dramatically as 'Breakdown' segues into 'The Great Disaster', the fastest and heaviest song on the record. The introduction has a great panning effect that shifts the tricky Brian May-style guitar acrobatics from left to right and provides a suitable dramatic opening that the rest of the track largely maintains. The anger of the lyrics is reflected in Clarkin's aggressive riffing and Stanway's restless piano chords and keyboard arpeggios. Of particular note is the almost funky acoustic guitar and bass interchange at 2.06, which leads into a wonderful keyboard break in prog/neo-prog style. This is a powerful hard rock track with that something extra that Magnum so often provide.

'Vicious Companions' (3:36)
Here's another song in a folky, hard rock vein, making good use of acoustic guitar and sampled strings. A low-key acoustic opening leads to an unusual shuffle propelled by an interlocking guitar and synth riff. Lowe's characterful bass line is a feature of the verses and there's another fabulous hooky chorus. There's also an unconscious homage to Ronnie James Dio, one of Catley's favourite vocalists, in the line, 'when everything's gone', at the end of the middle eight. Catley's vocals are probably even better in the Friday Rock Show session, but the overall recording lacks the album version's energy.

'So Far Away' (4:35)
This is more straight-ahead hard rock in terms of instrumentation, with the guitar doing the heavy lifting and the keyboard providing melodic embellishments and textures. The dramatic shift in time signature and volume into the 'so far away' section is an interesting idea, though it doesn't entirely come off and always sounds a little awkward. Lyrically, this is another song with an anti-war message along the lines of 'Soldier of the Line'. There are some cleverly constructed lyrics here that work well rhythmically with the music, such as, 'So please don't praise those mindless games/With reckless claims/Of glory and fame'.

'Hit And Run' (3:39)
One criticism made of *The Eleventh Hour* is that the second side of the vinyl is dominated by AOR or soft rock tracks. This seems to me both to underplay the quality of some of these songs and to misunderstand the development the band were making in integrating different elements of melodic rock. On 'Hit And Run', Clarkin seems to have been experimenting with writing melodies, instrumental hooks and lyrical themes that were more direct than his earlier

work. There's a hint of AC/DC in the guitar riff, the walking bass line and the swinging chords in the pre-chorus, while the keyboard-enhanced chorus is pure American FM rock. The main riff, meanwhile, is remarkably similar to the one Clarkin wrote for Sue McCloskey's 'I Really Need Your Love' single two years earlier. While Clarkin was to perfect his technique for constructing melodic rock tunes on future albums, 'Hit And Run' is a good track that doesn't sound out of place on the record.

'One Night Of Passion' (3:48)
This is a fairly dark song exploring the moral implications of a one-night stand. Musically, it's another track with a slow groove, with the rhythm section again prominent and Clarkin and Stanway providing the colour on top. It's a moody, involving piece, but it doesn't stick as long in the memory as the rest of the record.

'The Word' (4:54)
Clarkin's best ballad up to that point, 'The Word' might have been the first Magnum single to breach the UK Top 40 had Jet decided to release it. It's an expertly constructed song, building from Stanway's evocative piano and layering it with stately drums and bass, keyboards and vocal harmonies. Catley delivers the song's optimistic message of carrying on and fighting despite the difficulties life throws up – a theme Clarkin was to develop in later ballads – with controlled passion. The positive vision of the lyrics, summed up in lines such as 'Time is on your side', might seem a little cheesy, but there's no doubt they made an impression on younger rock fans during the 1980s, as Michael Anthony acknowledged in his semi-autobiographical book *Words And Music*.

An orchestrated version of the song, scored by ELO strings arranger Louis Clark, with the London Philharmonic Orchestra, was prepared for a single release that never happened. Strangely, the orchestra is quite low in the mix, a decision Clarkin recognised 'as a bit of a cock-up on my part' in the 2005 sleeve notes. This version finally emerged on the 'Just Like an Arrow' 12" single in 1985.

'Young And Precious Souls' (4:03)
This is an incredibly vibrant track that encapsulates much of what works about the album. Built on a pulsing drum beat and bass line, it's a joyous piece of music full of unexpected chord changes and shifts in volume and tempo. But at its heart is a fabulous series of melodies: the verse, pre-chorus and chorus are all effective individually, but the band bind them together effortlessly. Stanway's keyboard moods and licks are a significant presence, as on much of the album. Lyrically, it appears to be more optimistic than much of what precedes it, with lines such as, 'Your legacy waits, come on, take a hold', suggesting that there is hope for the future despite the album's overall

message of 'the parlous state of the world today' as Catley explained it to the music correspondent of the *Evening Sentinel* in May 1983.

'Road To Paradise' (3:30)

The Eleventh Hour concludes in confident style with this concise yet absorbing track that packs three great melodic sections into three and a half minutes. Indeed, the 'We're all spinning on the roundabout' and 'I don't wish to fight' sections are among the best on the album. The combination of strummed acoustic guitar and the odd flashy electric lick works a treat again, but as on much of the record, it's Stanway's keyboard that's responsible for the majority of the instrumental hooks. The power and clarity of Catley's vocal is another feature of the track, both on the album and Friday Rock Show versions. Although it's more upbeat than most of the album, 'Road To Paradise' ends in an ominous fashion as the music fades out to the sound of exactly 11 bell strikes.

Related Tracks
'Back To Earth' (3:37)

Recorded sometime in 1982 at Portland Studios, 'Back To Earth' was the lead studio track released as part of the *Live In America* EP in October 1982. It's a slice of high-energy hard rock that, with its driving electric guitar and galloping rhythm, resembles the material on *Chase The Dragon* rather more than the contemporaneous *The Eleventh Hour* tracks. A song that highlights Magnum's link with the more melodic side of the NWOBHM, 'Back to Earth' was a live favourite throughout the 1980s. It was the opening track on the 1988 *On The Wings Of Heaven Live* video/laserdisc and was chosen for the band's farewell tour in 1995.

'Hold Back Your Love' (3:18)

The second studio track on the *Live In America* EP, 'Hold Back Your Love' is a laid-back, AOR-infused tune with little to distinguish it from the competition. There are some tasty guitar phrases, but overall, it all seems a little laboured. It lacks the bite and energy of 'Back to Earth' and the more developed melodic rock tunes on *The Eleventh Hour*.

'True Fine Love' (3:22)

This is an enjoyable track that reveals Clarkin's liking for 1950s and 1960s rock 'n' roll. First released as part of the 1993 *Archive* set, the liner notes reveal it was left off *The Eleventh Hour* because it didn't align with the rest of the material. Certainly, it has more in common with the songs Clarkin was writing during the 1990s for *Rock Art* and his Hard Rain project when he was trying to break free from what he saw as the Magnum formula. Nonetheless, it's a well-written, catchy track that might at least have been used as a B-side for one of the *On A Storyteller's Night* singles.

On A Storyteller's Night (1985)

Personnel:
Tony Clarkin: all guitar and backing vocals
Bob Catley: lead vocals
Mark Stanway: all keyboards
Wally Lowe: bass and backing vocals
Jim Simpson: drums and percussion
Additional musicians:
Mo Birch: additional vocals on 'Les Morts Dansant'
Produced and engineered at The Abattoir Studios, Birmingham by Kit Woolven
Release date: 13 May 1985 on FM Records
Cover Design: Rodney Matthews
Highest chart places: UK: 24, West Germany: Did not chart, Sweden: 44
Running time: 45:45

If 1984 was Magnum's *annus horribilis*, that year also laid the roots for
the band's revival. Tony Clarkin had received the double blow of losing his
mother and being laid down by a serious illness in late 1983 and the band
was put on hiatus for three months. They returned for a club tour in February
and March 1984, with ex-Stampede guitarist Lawrence Archer providing
additional guitar. However, Clarkin's health took some time to improve and
with limited plans for future work, both Kex Gorin and Mark Stanway left
Magnum, the former to join Robin George's band and the latter teaming up
with Phil Lynott and Archer in Grand Slam.

The key development in the upturn of the band's fortunes was the arrival
of manager Keith Baker, a friend of Clarkin's, a former musician himself and
a local entrepreneur who had had some success in the fashion business.
Also added to the ranks were keyboard player Eddie George, who'd been a
member of future Black Sabbath vocalist Tony Martin's band The Alliance, and
drummer Jim Simpson, who had been playing in pop group Bloomsbury Set.
The concerts undertaken by this line-up in November and December 1984
proved vital in boosting the band's confidence. The tour, including a raft of
new songs from what was to become *On A Storyteller's Night*, was a make-
or-break one, as Clarkin recalled in a 2017 *Rock Candy* interview: 'We had no
clue whether the fans would be there for us. If the tour had gone badly, then
that would have been the end of Magnum'.

Clarkin recalls that the band began demoing new material around the
autumn of 1984, although it's possible some of the recordings included on
the 2005 expanded edition of *On A Storyteller's Night* were produced before
that, as Kex Gorin is credited on drums. Indeed, it's not entirely clear what
the precise line-up of the band was through much of 1984 and early 1985.
Stanway has claimed in his autobiography and elsewhere that he never
officially left the group in 1984, whereas Clarkin told *Rock Candy* that when
the keyboardist came back to replace Eddie George in March 1985, it was

on a session basis initially. This seems to be confirmed by press reports that referred to Magnum having been reduced to a nucleus of Catley, Clarkin and Lowe, with the other members listed as temporary touring musicians.

The album was recorded at The Abattoir Studios in Birmingham, which was owned by pop reggae act, UB40. It was preceded by a single – 'Just Like An Arrow' b/w 'Two Hearts' – produced by the band. However, the album was overseen by Kit Woolven, an experienced hard rock producer and engineer who had previously worked with Thin Lizzy. Clarkin praised both studio and producer in the 2005 album sleeve notes; in the latter case, particularly in terms of getting a great drum sound from Simpson's old battered kit. For Stanway, Woolven had both credibility and a range of clever recording techniques that the band hadn't experienced before. The sessions were financed by the band themselves and, like *Chase The Dragon*, the album was recorded fairly quickly – in less than a fortnight, in fact.

One major issue was that the band didn't have a record contract. 'I think we approached every record company in the country and they all turned us down' Clarkin told *Classic Rock*, with typical self-deprecation, in 2004. With no other offers on the table, Magnum signed a one-off deal with local Wolverhampton-based label FM Records.

Although *Storyteller's Night* marked a turning point in the band's fortunes, there was no radical reinvention of their sound. The more elaborate and involved tracks remained at the core of the record, but alongside these were a handful of succinct, melodic hard rock songs delivered with a newfound sharpness and economy. Not only had the level of songwriting moved up a gear, but there was barely a dip in quality across the album's ten tracks.

It also benefitted from being adorned with one of the best fantasy-based rock covers of all time. Rodney Matthews' illustration of a hooded figure (the storyteller of the title) lecturing to a motley collection of goblins and dwarves in a fire-lit tavern has become an iconic sleeve. As with *The Eleventh Hour*, the main idea was Clarkin's, but Matthews added a host of details, such as the mice on the ale barrel, the pictures of the last two album covers on the wall and his own dog lying on the floor. The scene was based on the interior of The George Inn in Norton St. Phillip, Somerset, close to where Matthews lived. It perfectly fits the mood and lyrics of the title track; an extraordinary achievement, especially as, up against a tight deadline, the artist completed it in a mere ten days.

Storytellers' Night did much better than *The Eleventh Hour*, reaching number 24 in the UK album charts. More significant, however, was the fact that with the help of Baker and FM Records, the band were getting more press and media attention than before, catapulting them from the margins to the centre of British hard rock. This resulted in a spot on the bill of the Monsters Of Rock festival at Donington Park on 17 August 1985, playing alongside Ratt, Metallica, Bon Jovi, Marillion and headliners ZZ Top. On the same day, the band signed a four-album deal with major label Polydor International, whose Head of A&R, Michael Golla, had been drawn to Magnum by the buzz around the latest record. Simpson had, by this time, left to join UFO and been replaced by Mickey Barker (born 12 January 1953), who was to remain on the drum stool for the next ten years.

'How Far Jerusalem' (6:26)

The album starts in fine style with this dark, atmospheric tune featuring great fantasy imagery but based on personal experiences. As Clarkin notes in the liner notes to the expanded edition:

> It was about us going to London, which is Britain's music capital, and so often coming back disappointed. You'd go down with demos and return thinking, 'What did we achieve?' So London was, in a sense, Jerusalem. Or it might as well have been.

The haunting vocal effect at the beginning of the track was achieved using reverse reverb, in which Catley's vocal was recorded with reverb before the reverb was taken away, reversed and applied to the front of each word instead. Stanway noted in an interview with the Australian *Sentinel Daily* web magazine that the track benefitted from connected layers of moody keyboards and the use of the new Yahama DX-7, with its vast range of sounds. But equally important was Clarkin's guitar, which provides the commanding riff at the heart of the song and the sparks and flourishes that elevate the finished version above the more pedestrian demo that can be heard on the expanded edition.

In moving between slow, almost ambient and raucous full-band sections, 'How Far Jerusalem' was not doing anything particularly new. Yet, as *Kerrang!* journalist Derek Oliver observed in hearing the song played live before the album's release, it was an incredibly ambitious composition, 'combining the best of Magnum's varied modes into one sensationally constructed epic'. Above all, it's a phenomenal piece of hard rock songwriting, with a chorus guaranteed to ensure hands in the air and pogoing in a live setting.

'How Far Jerusalem' is one of four songs on the album that have remained live favourites across the decades. It has often been extended to over ten minutes in concert, with space given over to instrumental noodling in the middle.

'Just Like An Arrow' (3:22)

Unpretentious and direct, 'Just Like An Arrow' signals more than any other track on the album how serious Magnum are about connecting to new and bigger audiences. It wasn't written as a potential hit, according to Clarkin, who has said it was put together very quickly with 'nothing premeditated about it'. Alongside the wonderful melody, the guitar and drum sound that Woolven achieved placed it firmly in the territory of American commercial rock. The conventional lyrical theme and the words themselves (with repetitions of the short verses) also suggest that Clarkin was aiming for simplicity. Despite this and a number of appearances on UK television, the single only made it to number 83 in the charts.

The single is quite different from the album version. The keyboards are more prominent and higher in the mix at the expense of the guitars. If you want a laugh, check out the bizarre video – the band sections were apparently filmed in a freezing quarry in Surrey – with an incomprehensible storyline involving a jeep, a bullring and a woman on a horse.

'On A Storyteller's Night' (4:59)

Clarkin wrote the title track on the tour bus during the group's six-week excursion around the UK in November/December 1984, after most of the album's other tunes had been penned. The basic idea, based on 'a mental image' Clarkin had 'of someone sitting around on a cold, windy night by an open fire', provided the inspiration for the fantasy-style lyrics and Matthews' cover. However, in common with the best of the guitarist's so-called 'sword and sorcery' compositions, there's a message based on realism at the core of the words. In particular, the lyrics to the chorus, and especially the 'Keep the night light burning' line, have emerged as something of a motto for the Magnum fanbase.

Musically, as elsewhere in the Magnum canon, changes in tempo and dynamics are a key feature. The song opens with synth textures, setting the mood for Catley's confident low-register vocal. It's not until 1.17 that the rest of the band enters for the storming but brief, chorus. From this point, the song builds slowly but majestically, with backing vocals added to the 'On a storyteller's night' refrain and then a double chorus that leads into an expertly executed guitar break at 3.05. Thereafter, the momentum never slips, Stanway's elegant keyboard fills augmenting the guitar attack and the rhythm section driving the song forward to its concise staged finish.

The main reason for its position near the very top of the hierarchy of Magnum songs is simply the richness of the melodies. Its haunting atmosphere and sheer melodic power have rarely failed to deliver in a live setting.

'Before First Light' (3:52)

Along with 'Just Like An Arrow', this was one of the first songs written for the album and was performed live during early 1984, although it then had the title, 'Through The Night'. The eventual title came from the headstone of a sea captain Clarkin had spotted when he was looking for lyrical inspiration, with the inscription, 'See you before first light'. Musically, it's one of the album's more concise and straightforward tunes. The song hangs on another striking guitar riff, around which Stanway paints enticing keyboard colours. The slowed-down chorus and partial instrumental dropout are interesting variations.

'Les Morts Dansant' (5:47)

This simply structured tune has grown to be considered a cornerstone in the Magnum catalogue over the years. It's a perfect example of the importance of fusing lyrics and music to create a piece greater than the sum of its parts. From early in the band's career, Clarkin allocated the lyrics equal importance to the music and, at times, has even said they are more important. 'Les Morts Dansant' is a case where the emotion associated with the subject matter, the delivery of the lyrics and the feeling of the music work in close harmony.

Inspired by a television documentary Clarkin had seen on the subject, this is an anti-war lyric with a twist. Originally titled 'Cannon', it focuses on the small but significant number of young British soldiers on the Western Front in the First World War who were executed for desertion and cowardice. Many of these were suffering from shell shock (now reclassified as Post Traumatic Stress Disorder or PTSD), which was little understood by army officials or medical professionals at the time. The title – literally translated from the French as 'The Dancing Dead' – refers to the movement of the body of the convicted man after being shot by the firing squad. Other details are historically accurate, such as the fact that the firing squad were always 'reluctant marksman' and the reference to the 'paper square to his heart pinned tight' to help ensure that death was quick.

'Les Morts Dansant' is a song that has developed and flourished through repeated concert airings over the decades. There's no doubt that the studio version lacks the power of some of the later live recordings. Part of this is down to the sound; Stanway has criticised the reedy keyboard sound as 'a bit twee' and, overall, the song certainly works better on live albums such as 1991's *The Spirit*. The final section, with Clarkin's 'Baba O'Riley' power chords, is especially engaging in concert, although it's worth remembering that the impact of the song's live outings is also due to Catley's reliably spectacular visual and vocal performance.

'Les Morts Dansant' was covered, albeit re-titled as 'Call To Heaven', rather effectively by American singer-songwriter Patty Smyth on her 1987 album, *Never Enough*. It was also adapted with new lyrics by Willie Nile for the song 'Bread Alone' on his 1999 album *Beautiful Wreck Of The World*.

'Endless Love' (4:30)

One of the overlooked gems on the album, 'Endless Love' is an example of the variety of compositional and production ideas woven around the album's less complex tracks. Of particular note is the tribal drumming that starts the song, the keyboard runs that dance on top of the main instrumentation and Lowe's powerful falsetto backing vocals. There's a depth to tracks such as 'Endless Love' that indicates that, even at their more commercial, Magnum were keen on ploughing similar furrows to bands like prog-AOR supergroup Asia, rather than their less thoughtful melodic rock contemporaries.

The demo is almost unrecognisable in parts; it has a different chorus, soulful female backing vocals and a few wayward synth effects. Overall, it sounds more like a (good) laid-back pop tune than a vigorous rock anthem.

'Two Hearts' (4:24)

Along with 'Just Like An Arrow', 'Two Hearts' is the most overtly commercial track on *Storyteller's Night*. After a brief opening with picked guitar and whirring synth effects, the song settles into a pure 1980s melodic rock groove with staccato riffing and extended keyboard chords. The synth sounds and twangy Dire Straits-style guitar licks may appear a little dated now, but the song does demonstrate how good Clarkin was at writing infectious pop-rock hooks. On stage, the guitar break between 2.37-3.20 was often extended to three or four minutes; as Clarkin joked in the 2005 sleeve notes: 'It was really only an excuse for me to do a long guitar solo and bore everyone to death!'

The earlier B-side sounds like a demo compared to the re-recorded album version. As well as having Clarkin singing the guitar refrain in the introduction, most of the guitar and keyboard embellishments that bring the song to life are missing. Without vocal harmonies, the chorus also lacks the aural punch of the final version.

'Steal Your Heart' (3:59)

Often overlooked due to the fact that it was not played live until the 2005 anniversary tour, 'Steal Your Heart' is another solid, melodic rock tune. It began life as 'Come On Young Love', with a different, slower but equally catchy chorus. The two demos included in the expanded edition outline the song's evolution from a mid-tempo ballad to a more dynamic, punchy, hard rock sing-a-long. All versions may be keyboard-heavy, but they're highlighted by some great soloing from Clarkin. While it's neither particularly profound nor complicated, 'Steal Your Heart' is great fun – Catley adds plenty of 'oohs', 'aahs' and 'babys' – and an indication that even the less celebrated songs on the album are far from fillers.

'All England's Eyes' (4:47)

The rhythm section of Simpson and Lowe star on the fourth *Storyteller's Night* track that has remained a regular in the setlist for decades. In what is otherwise a conventionally arranged song, the tribal drum rolls in the verses (missing from the demo), which are repeated during the massed gang vocals between 2.36-2.56 and the bridge to the keyboard break at 3.32, are incredibly effective. It's also a track that demonstrates the delicate balance the band achieved on this album between guitar and keyboards; Stanway's moody chords offset Clarkin's rhythmic riffing and crunchy hook lines. The keyboardist tended not to have too many solos; thus, the simple, anthemic keyboard section between 3.32-4.06 is another welcome addition.

'All England's Eyes' is a very good song that, as with 'Les Morts Dansant', has been lifted to a higher level in the live setting over the years. The opportunity it affords for audience participation means that, as Stanway noted, 'it always went down as one of the best live'.

'The Last Dance' (3:43)

The final track on *Storyteller's Night* is this ballad that nearly wasn't a ballad. The demo (included in the expanded edition) is an uptempo tune with a galloping rhythm but is otherwise very similar to the final version. Stanway has noted that he worked on a piano part that turned the song into a slow ballad, an idea that Clarkin liked. According to Stanway, he also worked with Woolven to record 'keyboard simulations of strings one track at a time', layering the piece as if it were the string section of an orchestra. 'Those were the days', the keyboardist told *Sentinel Daily* in 2022, 'when I had more input'.

The faster version is actually pretty effective, but there's no doubt that in slowing it down, the band gave the track a distinctive twist. The lyrics also seem to work better attached to a ballad. Clarkin recalled in 2005 that he 'was thinking of the old days when dances took place in village halls and you'd have formally to request a partner to take the floor with you. It was a semi-romantic vision, I suppose'.

Certain reviewers loved 'The Last Dance'. Derek Oliver in *Kerrang!* considered it, along with 'Two Hearts', 'the best song ... Magnum have ever penned' and a potential hit single. Whereas Oliver praised the simple use of 'piano, voice and pockets of silence', it isn't a song that has aged particularly well. The band would certainly go on to produce ballads that were better and less schmaltzy than this.

Vigilante (1986)

Personnel:
Tony Clarkin: guitar and backing vocals
Bob Catley: lead vocals
Mark Stanway: keyboards
Wally Lowe: bass guitar and backing vocals
Mickey Barker: drums
Additional musicians:
Roger Taylor: backing vocals on 'When The World Comes Down' and 'Sometime Love'
Daniel Bourquin: saxophone on 'Midnight (You Won't Be Sleeping)'
Produced at Mountain Studios, Montreux, Switzerland by Roger Taylor and Dave Richards
Engineer: Dave Richards
Release date: 26 September 1986 on Polydor Records
Cover Illustration: Chris Moores
Highest chart places: UK: 24, West Germany: 59, Sweden: 16
Running time: 43:36

There was a lot of change for Magnum in the recording of their first album for a major label. Recognising the commercial potential of the band, Polydor International gave them a free choice of producer and studio. Clarkin's publishing company Tritec sent out demo tapes, including versions of 'Back Street Kid', 'Red On The Highway' and 'Lonely Night', to a number of high-profile producers. Most responded positively, but the band opted for Queen drummer Roger Taylor and engineer/producer Dave Richards. As well as co-producing Taylor's solo albums *Fun In Space* (1981) and *Strange Frontier* (1984), Richards had recently engineered and co-produced Chris Rea's *On The Beach*, Iggy Pop's *Blah-Blah-Blah* and Queen's *A Kind Of Magic* (all released in 1986). The added advantage of going with Taylor and Richards was that the band were able to record at Queen's luxurious Mountain Studios on the banks of Lake Geneva in Montreux, Switzerland.

Beginning in May 1986, the recording of *Vigilante* is remembered more fondly by most of the band than the two subsequent albums with Polydor. With lots of promotional work to do with Queen, Taylor wasn't present throughout the three months of recording; indeed, Richards noted in a 1989 *Sound On Sound* interview that Taylor effectively 'left it to me'. However, Catley and Clarkin recall Taylor's involvement positively, noting that he came up with plenty of ideas for improving the songs. Speaking to *Kerrang!* in October 1986, Lowe observed that Taylor had been instrumental in varying the programme of recording so that all members of the band were kept on their toes and not left 'sitting around twiddling our fingers' after completing their contributions.

Overall, the album boasts a more modern production than previous Magnum records, with greater use of effects and a punchier drum sound.

This is particularly true of the remixed versions of the singles that have a trademark 1980s production. Richards noted that it was generally a live setup in the studio but with great use of the available technology. At the time of release, Clarkin praised the production as a huge step forward from previous albums. He told *Metal Hammer* in October 1986 that he was delighted with the polished sound, as opposed to what he considered a fashionable preference for 'street-level production' that sounds 'like a pile of crap'. By the time of *Wings Of Heaven*, however, Clarkin had become more critical, in particular, in relation to the mix, where he felt the keyboards had been overdone at the expense of the guitars.

While the lyrical themes of the album didn't seem markedly dissimilar from *Storyteller's Night,* Clarkin also claimed that there'd been an overhaul in subject matter to more earthly concerns. As he told *Kerrang!*'s Malcolm Dome:

> I got as far as I could with my traditional writing method and I just felt it was time to change direction. I believe I had to introduce more realism into my words… We could either ignore the world outside and just carry on regardless or else take a chance and move on. There really is no substitute for the latter, is there?

Clarkin also thought that there was an air of optimism – 'a positive vibe' in his words – underpinning much of the material, maybe because, as he noted in a June 1986 *Kerrang!* interview, he was able to pull back the curtains to look across a lake 'at a huge bloody mountain every morning'.

The modernisation of the band also extended to their image. Manager Keith Baker pressed the band members to tidy themselves up, introduced stylists and generally encouraged them to think more carefully about the way they presented themselves onstage and in the press. Before Baker's intervention, Catley noted in a *Sounds* feature in October 1986, 'the idea of the band as *an image* never really entered our heads'.

There's little doubt that Magnum were anxious to broaden their appeal to the widest possible audience. Despite being well supported by publications such as *Kerrang!* and *Metal Hammer,* they were eager to position themselves as a rock band and distance themselves from associations with heavy metal. This went as far as the album title, which Clarkin, in particular, was anxious should be as neutral as possible so as not to alienate potential record buyers. Whether the chosen title and sleeve achieved this is open to debate, although the striking new logo is a clear steer away from heavy metal and reflects a more modernist approach.

As far as the cover was concerned, the intention had been to keep Rodney Matthews on board. Matthews forwarded a design (included in 'The Ones That Got Away' page of his website) based on Clarkin's general concept. It featured a unicorn bounding across a chequerboard background with some form of armoured vehicle in the distance. Aside from the purple and pink sky, the design was a striking black and white. Polydor, however, decided to go with science fiction artist Chris Moores' alternative illustration of a unicorn (meant to symbolise peace) in a pink marble room with a black rock about to transform into the evil entity that Clarkin had seen in a dream and insisted was included on the cover. Moores wasn't impressed with Clarkin's idea but agreed to do it, adding the whirlpool, the mountain range and the spiral galaxy in the background. The final cover is as much of a mess as the description above suggests. Its association with one of Magnum's best-loved albums may have saved it from some criticism, but it's surely one of the band's worst sleeves.

That *Vigilante* only matched *Storyteller's Night* in reaching number 24 in the UK album charts was something of a disappointment for the band. The failure of the album's three singles in the UK ('Need A Lot of Love' was additionally released in France and West Germany) also perturbed the record company, who were particularly frustrated that the main national pop music station, BBC Radio 1, refused to play the band's songs. Yet, there was considerable progress in other directions. As well as playing huge festival dates supporting Marillion in the UK and Status Quo and Jethro Tull in continental Europe, a lengthy European tour was organised on the back of creditable positions in the German (number 58) and Swedish (number 16) charts. A second European jaunt in March and April 1987 included visits to Belgium, the Netherlands, France, Italy, Austria, Denmark and Switzerland as well as the UK, Germany and Sweden. Rooted in the successful 1978 dates supporting Whitesnake in West Germany, Magnum's popularity in mainland Europe was beginning to blossom.

'Lonely Night' (3:48)
Vigilante opens with its most heavily produced and blatantly commercial tune. Driven along by a prominent crisp drum sound and squelchy synth bass, Taylor and Richards add a host of melodic touches and effects. By and large, these enhance the song's appeal, but in places – such as the harsh rhythmic additions in the chorus – they distract from the tune's basic structure. In the final minute, the simple melody is allowed to cut through and the song soars. The bouncy, upbeat mood hides the dark tale of loneliness and isolation at the core of the lyric: lines such as 'I can't take this heartbreak' and 'I'm feeling so empty/In this old crazy world tonight' leave little room for misinterpretation.

The band may have chosen 'Lonely Night' as the first track on the album and the lead single because it was familiar to fans, having been played at the Christmas shows in 1985. An extended version of over five minutes released on the 12" single includes additional studio effects but adds nothing substantial to the song. Despite the weight thrown behind it, the single only reached number 70 in the UK charts.

'Need A Lot Of Love' (4:46)

One of the musical highpoints of the album, 'Need A Lot Of Love' also incorporates a poignant lyric reflecting Magnum's supposed new grounded realism. A survey of international trouble spots in the mid-1980s – from Lebanon to Berlin and Belfast – this is Clarkin as a social and political commentator, succinctly summing up an everyman's view of the state of the world (the idea may have come from Barclay James Harvest's 1974 track, 'Child Of The Universe'). Some of the lines in the song are among his most powerful: 'Smoking in a room in Lebanon/The hotel's serving, but the hospital's gone'. Not surprisingly, reactions to the song were heightened when the band played it in Northern Ireland or West Germany. Interestingly, the track seems to have been titled 'Saigon' (reflecting the first verse's reference to the city, now known as Ho Chi Minh City, at the heart of the Vietnam War) up until the very last minute. The change was perhaps made in order to make it appear less overtly political and to emphasise the universal sentiments in the chorus.

The song is characterised not only by an impressive melodic range but also by the clever juxtaposition of the solemn refrain of the verse and the simple but effective ascending and descending tune in the chorus. Here, the clarity of the production accentuates the song's punchy rhythm to deliver one of the most immediate songs Magnum have ever produced. The remixed version released for the French and German markets in 1987 has a handful of additional guitar parts that work really effectively.

'Sometime Love' (4:20)

Drifting synth chords segue into this lively pop-rock track. Although it's not among the album's highlights, 'Sometime Love' is another song that shows off the production tricks Taylor and Richards bring to the table. Synth stabs, isolated guitar licks and backward tracking punctuate what is a fairly unremarkable tune. Once again, the big, bright drum sound and prominent rhythm track are notable, as are the massed backing vocals, which on this occasion include Taylor himself.

'Midnight (You Won't Be Sleeping)' (4:01)

Written in Switzerland in a couple of days, 'Midnight' is Clarkin developing his compositional technique and parading his melodic flair. The lilting acoustic guitar opening may have been left to develop organically on earlier albums, but here it is bolstered by a rigid drum beat and a warm bass run driving forward towards the sensational chorus. Here, underpinned by dynamic power chords, Catley's vocal climbs to help create one of Clarkin's most effective earworms to date. The saxophone solo is an unusual and slightly unexpected bonus. Different views exist as to how it was put together. Lowe claimed in *Kerrang!* that the elderly jazz saxophonist 'knocked it out virtually off-the-cuff', whereas Stanway's account in his autobiography was that the solo was pieced together by Richards through a sampler because the session musician hadn't produced a useable solo.

Released as the album's second single in October 1986 (with 'Back Street Kid' on the reverse), there was plenty of hope for 'Midnight'; *Sounds* judged it to be 'a crisp, rather classy follow-up to 'Lonely Night', the sort of tune that threatens to make [Magnum]... outrageously popular'. Unfortunately, it only reached number 96. The six-minute remix on the 12" (an edited version was included on the 7" format), was considered strong enough to be put on the 1993 *Chapter And Verse* and 2010 *The Gathering* compilations.

'Red On The Highway' (4:14)
Written and performed as early as 1985, this is a thunderous hard rock track that makes excellent use of the album's huge drum sound. Clarkin's heavy riffing is all over the song, but equally important are Barker's insistent and punchy rhythms that consistently cut through the mix. In such a heavy track, it might not be surprising for the keyboards to disappear, but Stanway is handed one of his few keyboard solos, a searing performance that lasts from 3.02-3.40.

'Holy Rider' (5:17)
The second side of the vinyl begins where the first left off, with a heavy rocker powered by whip-like drums and taut guitar riffs. Unlike 'Red On The Highway', however, 'Holy Rider' is a complex beast with a number of contrasting sections and a range of dynamics. The first section – a sparse, syncopated rock anthem – is fine, but the song really gets interesting from the 'Down from the hills' section that leads into the chorus with its powerful 'Heart of stone' refrain. Taylor and Richards pepper the song with a number of vocal and instrumental effects which really come into their own during the downbeat instrumental section from 2.39-3.40, parts of which are reminiscent of some of the more atmospheric passages on Marillion's 1985 album *Misplaced Childhood*. The title and some of the lyrics may allude to Christian messaging, in particular the prophet Ezekiel's reference to God removing the heart of stone within people and replacing it with a heart of flesh, thus making them spiritually alive.

'When The World Comes Down' (5:20)
This is the best ballad Clarkin has ever written and has a claim to be considered one of the greatest ballads in 1980s hard rock. It's emotionally raw but carries none of the gushing sentimentality of your average American soft rock narrative. As befits a band like Magnum and the struggles they'd endured up to this point, it's not a song about love but about dealing with life's setbacks, loneliness and (possibly) depression. Despite the disturbing images of someone hiding 'out of sight', 'feeling so small' and crying to themselves, the song ultimately offers hope in the idea that despite the whole

world seeming to 'come down on you', it might 'shine on you tomorrow' and your dreams could 'come true'.

Clarkin explained on the *Black Country Music Show* in 2011 how the track was transformed from a much slower dirge-like demo. The band recorded their parts, but then Richards added 'a pile of keyboards' and echo effects. Also crucial to the final sound were the massed harmonies in the chorus and the thoughtful use of synth flute and pulsing 10CC-esque keyboards. Clarkin was delighted with the treatment the track had been given, applauding it in *Kerrang!* as a passionately sung epic, a bit 'like a national anthem'. The edited 7" version cuts out an instrumental section after the first chorus and truncates the ending.

'Vigilante' (6:40)

A storming live track, 'Vigilante' has been played on stage more often than any other Magnum song. The studio version is equally impressive. It's a heavy guitar-dominated song but it also displays subtlety and maturity and benefits from the studio effects the producers were experimenting with at Mountain Studios.

Moody keyboards introduce a catchy, winding guitar riff around which Catley delivers a raspy vocal. At 43 seconds, Clarkin brings in the main guitar theme, followed by the 'Go call the vigilante' pre-chorus. It's already tremendous stuff, but the bar is raised further by the simply scintillating chorus, augmented by the most powerful harmonised vocals the band had recorded up to that point. Special note should be made of Lowe's melodious driving bass line and the delicate use of what sounds like a haunting background choir in the song's final minute. 'Vigilante' wasn't released as a single, but a special recording of the band performing the song was shown on Channel 4's popular music show, *The Tube*, in the UK in April 1987.

'Back Street Kid' (5:01)

Vigilante ends with another song that had already become a favourite in the live set. 'Back Street Kid' is a fairly hackneyed tale of an aspiring musician and his dreams of making the big time. Musically, we're also in conventional rock territory, with a simple chanted chorus that repeats rather too much towards the end and a basic chord sequence that sounds a little like Van Halen's classic, 'Jump'. Stanway is centre-stage again here, offloading a number of keyboard motifs and playful piano arpeggios. *Kerrang!*'s Malcolm Dome noted that there'd been a remarkable guitar solo in the demo, which was 'spliced out' of the final version.

Wings Of Heaven (1988)

Personnel:
Tony Clarkin: guitar and backing vocals
Bob Catley: lead vocals
Mark Stanway: keyboards
Wally Lowe: bass guitar and backing vocals
Mickey Barker: drums
Additional musicians:
Attie Bauw: Fairlight programming
The London Gospel Choir: backing vocals on 'It Must Have Been Love'
Max Werner: backing vocals on 'Different Worlds'
Produced at Wisseloord Studios, The Netherlands by Albert Boekholt and
Magnum except 'Days Of No Trust' produced at Sarm West Studios, UK by Joe
Barbaria
Mixed at Sarm West Studios, UK, by Joe Barbaria and Ross Cullum
Release date: 28 March 1988 on Polydor Records
Cover Photography: Paul Cox
Highest chart places: UK: 5, West Germany: 19, Sweden: 2
Running time: 44:07

Magnum's seventh studio album, *Wings Of Heaven*, represented the high
point of the band's commercial success. It stormed to number five in the
UK album charts (and was certified silver – representing over 60,000 sales –
within three weeks of release), made number two in Sweden and reached as
high as 19 in West Germany, where their profile was rapidly rising. Even more
impressively, it spawned three Top-40 UK singles (including a *Top Of The Pops*
appearance), broadening the band's mainstream appeal and opening the door,
or so Polydor believed, for them to become a major crossover rock act on a
par with Bon Jovi and Whitesnake.

In concert, the set, lights and sound had all become bigger and Magnum
moved to larger venues, such as Birmingham's NEC Arena. They were also
now cover stars in the British rock press and, despite the occasional dig at
their age, received substantial support from publications such as *Kerrang!*,
Metal Hammer and *Raw*. For David Galbraith in *Kerrang!*, Magnum's
'triumphant' Christmas 1988 shows had 'proved them to be the brightest stars
in the firmament'.

For all its eventual success, the recording of *Wings Of Heaven* was far from
smooth. The original plan had been to work with Roger Taylor again and
possibly record at Ibiza Sound Studio. Eventually, however, the band gathered
at Phonogram's Wisseloord studio complex in Hilversum in the Netherlands
in late 1987. Wisseloord was one of the most in-demand studios in Western
Europe, with Def Leppard, Elton John, ELO and Tina Turner among recent
clients. Catley and Clarkin recalled in a 2022 *Fireworks* article that while
it was a fantastic studio, they were unhappy with the chosen producer,

Dutchman Albert Boekholt, and the recording process: 'It was just so time-consuming', Clarkin noted. Lowe explained to *Kerrang!* in February 1988 that the drums and bass had been recorded digitally to give the tracks a punchy bottom end. For Barker, it meant having to play all the drum parts into the Fairlight sequencer and then overdub the cymbals separately. In his autobiography, Stanway remembered it as 'an arduous process'.

Returning to the UK at Christmas, the band were dissatisfied with the Wisseloord recordings: 'We couldn't listen to what we'd done', Catley recalled, 'It was rubbish'. The band employed two established producers to help rescue the album. Joe Barbaria, who had worked with The Cars, was brought in to do a new production job on the first single, 'Days Of No Trust', and to mix the more commercial tracks – the other singles plus 'Different Worlds'. Ross Cullum, who had mixed and co-produced Tears for Fears and Wang Chung, among others, came in to mix the heavier, more atmospheric tracks. Both were working simultaneously at Trevor Horn's Sarm West Studios in London.

The final production does a great job of combining the intricate elements of Magnum's sound with a more commercial melodic rock approach. Although Clarkin has tended to dismiss the album's 'pop sound', the indiscriminate use of technology and, in particular, the 'horrible' sound of the guitars and snare drum, *Wings Of Heaven* is in many respects the most ambitious of the band's 1980s albums. In 'Wild Swan' and 'Don't Wake The Lion', it includes two elaborately constructed epics that, unlike some of the earlier proggy tracks in the catalogue, have an immediate melodic appeal. Taken together, the material included on the album and the single B-sides amount to the finest collection of songs Clarkin had written.

A number of alternative titles were suggested before the final choice was made. For some time, the band favoured *Different Worlds*, even to the point where manager Keith Baker had begun planning a stage set around the theme. *Don't Wake The Lion* was also an option but was ultimately rejected for being a little too insular when the band were hoping to expand their appeal internationally. According to Martin Vielhaber in his online biography, the more prosaic *Magnum* and *Magnum '88* were also considered. Ultimately, the band chose *Wings Of Heaven*, drawn from one of the most poetic lines in 'Wild Swan': 'Out to sea on the wings of heaven/Where silver cuts like a knife'.

The cover is the only Magnum album to feature an image of the band. The photograph of the band standing on a desolate rocky landscape was taken by experienced rock lensman Paul Cox, who had previously photographed the band for the inside sleeve of *Marauder*. The red and yellow design is striking, but it's a fairly generic 1980s cover, closely following the blueprint of U2's *The Joshua Tree*. Catley justified it at the time in terms of the band 'constantly looking for something different', although one shouldn't rule out the influence of Polydor in opting for a more commercial, modern and less heavy metal-style image to help sell the album.

Unusually, Clarkin provided a fairly detailed account of the inspiration behind the songs on *Wings Of Heaven* in the 1988 spring tour programme around the time of the album's release.

'Days Of No Trust' (5:23)

The first single from the album, this is an evergreen Magnum tune merging soaring harmonies with a big production sound. With its chiming keyboard riff and bouncing rhythm, there's always been a feel-good element to the song, although there's no shortage of clever compositional touches. The key change going into the verse, in particular, is simply sublime and the understated keyboard outro adds to the song's air of mystery. Moreover, Clarkin's guitars sound bright and raw, steering things along in a commanding style above the wash of keyboards.

Part of 'Days Of No Trust' was written during the mixing of *Vigilante* in the summer of 1986 and was first played live at the Reading Festival in August 1987. A reflection on the failure of politicians – and people more generally – to deal with the big problems in the world by deceiving themselves and telling 'the same old lies', Clarkin's programme notes also suggest the song can be read as a statement on the ultimate futility of the Reagan-Gorbachev missile reduction talks taking place at the time. The line, 'Headlines are courted by stretch limousines', was a dig at the behaviour of the band themselves during the *Vigilante* tour.

Backed by 'Maybe Tonight', the edited single (minus the introduction, second verse and outro) reached number 32 in the UK charts. Clarkin was never totally satisfied with the original and, in 2021, had 'a second crack at recording it the way that I imagined it to be'. This version, with a new introduction and a few added keyboard parts, was included on the bonus disc of *The Monster Roars* and opened the set at each of Magnum's 2022 live dates.

'Wild Swan' (6:15)

'Wild Swan' is not only one of Magnum's greatest songs but is among the very best hard rock tracks of the 1980s. It is built around a rip-snorting labyrinthine Led Zeppelin-style riff and a booming rhythm section. On top of this are layered vocals that narrate a twisting tale of flight and freedom, dripping with emotion. Catley's versatility here is mesmerising. In fact, it's difficult to pinpoint a song on which he has ever sounded better.

It's an expertly structured song. Opening with a heavy guitar-dominated section, at 1.10, it shifts into the 'Fly home/It's just me and you' part, a fabulous shuffle held down by Lowe's probing bass line and some elegant guitar harmonies. At 2.36, the shuffle breaks down into a ballad section, with the refrains of the earlier sections repeated at half speed. The emotional intensity of the final three minutes is enhanced by atmospheric keyboards, piercing guitar licks and some of Clarkin's most concise and powerful lyrics.

The idea for the song came, as was often the case, from a television programme showing birds flying despite having been hit by crossbow bolts. Clarkin built a 'fairy tale' around this image concerning 'the search for safety, following the river down to the sea and then on to an imaginary safe place'. In its focus on the search for some form of escape from the horrifying realities of life, Clarkin envisaged it as a companion piece to 'Days Of No Trust'.

'Start Talking Love' (3:36)

Although it's Magnum's highest charting UK single, reaching number 22 in May 1988, 'Start Talking Love' never really buried itself into the hearts of the band or the fanbase. In an article entitled 'Metal Goes Pop', the academic Benjamin Earl has suggested that with its simplistic, cliché-ridden lyrics (which he even claims echo Rick Astley's number one smash from 1987, 'Never Gonna Give You Up') and light instrumentation, 'Start Talking Love' was 'more a pop than a rock song'. Clarkin and Catley have similarly dismissed the song as exemplifying what they saw as *Wings Of Heaven*'s pop sound. Certainly, Clarkin found the song easier to write than usual. He recalls that the core of the track came from him, Lowe and Catley messing about in a spare studio at Wisseloord and that the music for the chorus was composed 'in about 20 seconds there and then'. Despite this, 'Start Talking Love' is more than a throwaway pop-rock confection. It's actually a carefully crafted piece of work, founded on a solid Lowe bass line, a simple Clarkin riff and a decent tune. The extended remix on the 12" and CD has some surprisingly nice touches, revealing a delicacy that's less evident on the album version.

'One Step Away' (4:39)

It says something about the quality of *Wings Of Heaven* that this cracking tune is one of its least celebrated tracks. It begins in an atmospheric fashion, with haunting guitar and vocal effects and great bass licks. But it soon develops into an outstanding slice of mid-paced AOR, Catley providing well-timed rock grunts and Clarkin a marvellously unrestrained guitar solo into the fade out. The fantasy lyric involving 'some evil spirit tempting a person to come with them' is less impressive and includes one of Clarkin's more tortuous couplets: 'Time has no respect for man's vanity/We hold the keys we are the caretakers of insanity'.

'It Must Have Been Love' (5:16)

This album's requisite ballad, 'It Must Have Been Love', was played live during the 1987 spring tour because it was apparently the easiest of the new songs for the band to learn. This early version, broadcast live on Tommy Vance's Radio 1 Friday Rock Show on 13 March 1987, is sparse, uncluttered and deeply emotional. The album version adds a lot of instrumentation, including a slightly overbearing staccato guitar refrain in the verse and keyboard embellishments across the track. It also features the London Gospel

Choir in a gargantuan power ballad chorus. This version still sounds great, but somehow, the extra buff and polish removes some of the tension and vulnerability suggested by the thinner keyboard sound and the isolated vocal of the earlier performance. The band continued to think the song worked best live. As Clarkin revealed in the *Goodnight LA* tour programme notes, when played live, 'I'd get a shiver down my spine, which just doesn't happen when you listen to the recorded version'.

'It Must Have Been Love' b/w 'Crying Time' was the third single from the album to make the UK Top 40, reaching number 33 in June 1988.

'Different Worlds' (4:39)

One of the album's more commercial tracks, 'Different Worlds' is based on an irresistibly catchy keyboard and guitar riff that bounds along with terrific energy. Clarkin is all over this one, with punchy riffs, a few heavy licks and some great soloing adding to the glossy sheen of the keyboard tracks. Barker's fiery drumming also raises the bar. As is true across the record, Catley's vocals are both powerful and expressive. For Clarkin, however, who seemed almost to disown the song as soon as it was released, there was an uncomfortable disconnect between the playful character of the music and the seriousness of the lyrics. Based on his experiences while on holiday in Nice in the south of France, where he witnessed people in extreme poverty living in close quarters to those with conspicuous wealth, the lyrics are a reasonable, if rather simplistic, attempt to convey what the guitarist considered to be an important social issue. But, as he communicated in an interview with *Raw* in December 1988, Clarkin found it 'practically impossible' to make the song convincingly carry the messages he'd intended and ultimately felt that it 'didn't work properly' and had 'failed'. The band's lack of love for 'Different Worlds' may explain the rather lacklustre rendition included on the *Wings Of Heaven Live* album in 2008.

'Pray For The Day' (3:45)

The penultimate song on the album is Clarkin's heartfelt reflection on the horrors associated with the Berlin Wall. According to his programme notes, he had the idea for the lyrics at an Austrian ski lodge high in the mountains (which explains the line, 'On top of the world nothing breaks in'). 'Cross after cross' references the churches Clarkin saw 'all with wrought iron crosses' and 'black ribbons and gauze hanging off'. In the songwriter's mind, this connected with the crosses along the Berlin Wall, marking the places where those trying to escape across the border to the West had been killed. Ultimately, it's a hopeful lyric, with Clarkin praying that one day the Wall (which he summarises in the laconic phrase 'concrete for chains') will 'crumble and fall'. The music beautifully conveys the sentiment in the words; atmospheric keyboard textures lead the way into another cracking riff and a beguiling, almost nursery rhyme-like, melody.

'Don't Wake The Lion (Too Old To Die Young)' (10:34)

The epic to end all Magnum epics, this, as the title suggests, is really two songs bolted together. Clarkin recalls in his programme notes that the first section was written while on tour in West Germany. The first line is inspired by Robb Wilton, a popular Lancashire comedian of the 1930s and 1940s famous for his monologues and, in particular, the catchphrase, 'The day war broke out...', which prompted Clarkin to develop a lyric about the futility of war as seen from both sides. He summarised his approach in an interview with Malcolm Dome in December 1988:

> Don't you think it's frightening that a group of faceless generals and politicians can sit in a room somewhere and draw a line on a map, then send out millions of young people to die in defence of that line without *anyone* ever explaining *why* this line is so important?! It's the futility I object to. What a waste. I come from a generation who don't want others to forget about such horrors.

While most of the references seem to be to the First World War, the allusion to the 'Maginot Line' (built by France in the 1930s to deter a future German invasion) suggests Clarkin also had the Second World War in mind.

The 'Too Old To Die Young' section, written in Dublin in the dressing room of the SFX Hall, was inspired by Clarkin accepting that it was now too late for him to 'die young' and 'have a good-looking corpse like James Dean'. He then took the general idea and applied it to the loss of life on the front line in a 20th-century war.

The song moves through a number of moods and tones, each section developing the musical narrative. The main 'Don't Wake The Lion' theme bookends the track: the first rendition, until around 2.40, is solemn and funereal; the closing portion from 7.50, meanwhile, is aggressive and urgent. The transitional section from 2.40-4.51 is dark and doomy, with some great effects, including operatic singing and sections from the Lord's Prayer. Barker's metronomic drumming ensures the momentum is never allowed to slip, providing a continuity to the 'Too Old' section, which includes some of Clarkin's most expressive guitar parts.

'Don't Wake The Lion' is one of Magnum's greatest achievements. Structurally reminiscent of some of the band's early work, it also sounds modern and of its time. Above all, it's full of passion and grit, with high-quality musicianship and a plethora of melodic hooks.

Related Tracks
'Maybe Tonight' (4:39)
Clarkin was at a songwriting high during the 1980s. It's no exaggeration to say that the three *Wings Of Heaven* B-sides would have been lead tracks on many melodic rock records at the time. The best of the three, 'Maybe Tonight'

could easily have been an A-side itself. It boasts one of the most instant melodic hooks in any Magnum verse and an equally memorable chorus. Included in the tracklisting up to a couple of months before the album's release, it was eventually relegated to the B-Side of 'Days Of No Trust'. It did feature on the US release of *Wings Of Heaven*, however, sandwiched between 'Pray For The Day' and 'Don't Wake The Lion'.

'C'est La Vie' (4:13)
The B-side to 'Start Talking Love', this was also included on the UK picture disc edition of the album. It's another tuneful hard rock track of the highest quality, doused in uplifting keyboards and with a handful of scorching guitar breaks. There's a hint of symphonic rock in the arrangement, with some lovely interchange between synth strings and guitar towards the end.

'Crying Time' (4:47)
Along with 'It Must Have Been Love', for which it was the B-side, this was written during the *Vigilante* sessions but never completed. Recorded with the Munich Philharmonic Orchestra at Union Studios in the city while the band was on tour in May 1988, and produced by Clarkin, it includes a full orchestral arrangement. A fairly simple ballad, 'Crying Time' is another track which might easily – in this or a more conventional form – have been a standout track on a less accomplished album.

Goodnight LA (1990)

Personnel:
Tony Clarkin: guitars and background vocals
Bob Catley: lead vocals
Mark Stanway: keyboards
Wally Lowe: bass guitar and background vocals
Mickey Barker: drums
Additional musicians:
Tommy Funderbunk and Michael Sadler: background vocals
Paulinho da Costa: percussion
Deric Dyer: saxophone
Mark Stanway and Jim Crichton: keyboard and computer programming
Produced and engineered at Goodnight LA Studios, Los Angeles, US by Keith Olsen
Assistant engineer: Shay Baby
Release date: 24 July 1990 on Polydor Records
Cover Design: Hugh Syme
Highest chart places: UK: 9, West Germany: 21, Sweden: 7
Running time: 48:40

> We want to break the American market; let's not pretend otherwise. We want to break new boundaries. It's called ambition.
> Tony Clarkin talking to Andy Bradshaw, *Metal Hammer*, 2-15 July 1990

The follow-up to *Wings Of Heaven* is one of the most controversial albums in the Magnum catalogue. Sometimes seen as the record where the band took a punt on accessing the American market but failed, it signalled the beginning of their commercial slide. Yet it still went Top Ten in the UK and Sweden, as well as making the Top 20 in Norway and Switzerland, and a creditable number 21 in Germany. The inclusion of writing collaborations and a number of overtly commercial tunes was seen by some in the UK music press as diluting the traditional Magnum sound. Ultimately, however, it's disappointing mainly in the sense that the songs aren't quite of the same standard as the previous three records.

Clarkin began writing the bulk of the material for the album in 1988. He demoed songs with Lowe and Catley at Soundcheck Studios in Birmingham, supervised by engineer Malcolm Ball and by December, had almost an album's worth of material. A selection was recorded with the whole band and sent out to prospective producers. Clarkin was hoping to have the album completed by the middle of 1989, but this was delayed when they convinced American producer Keith Olsen to oversee the record. Olsen was, at the time, one of the biggest names in transatlantic rock, having produced Whitesnake's best-selling album, *1987*, as well as records by Foreigner, Pat Benatar and Ozzy Osbourne. But it was hearing Rick Springfield's 1988 *Rock Of Life* album that convinced Clarkin that Olsen was the man for the job, although Magnum had to wait another year to secure his services.

In the meantime, as well as rehearsing and honing the material, Clarkin supplemented it by co-writing a number of additional songs with some of the best-known songsmiths in the field of melodic rock. Encouraged by manager Keith Baker, Clarkin's first choice of collaborator was Russ Ballard, the former singer and guitarist with Argent, who had had songs covered by Rainbow and Kiss, among others. Clarkin wrote four songs with Ballard, three of which appeared on the album. A fourth song called 'Dancing With The Devil' didn't make the record. Clarkin also travelled to California to work with Sue Shifrin, who'd written for Tina Turner, Heart and Meat Loaf, among others, with whom he wrote three songs. He then went to Vancouver and completed two songs over four days from 30 October to 2 November 1989 with Jim Vallance, who was best known for his work with Bryan Adams. A song apiece from the Shifrin and Vallance writing sessions made it onto the album.

After the release of *Wings Of Heaven*, Magnum had been inherited by Polydor UK (after Polydor International ceased to exist) and Clarkin felt there were few people at the label who understood the band. He has frequently noted in interviews that the label wanted Magnum to become Def Leppard or Whitesnake and that they were told to aim to sell two million copies of the next album. As a result, Clarkin felt pressured into collaborating with outside writers, although he seems to have kept those concerns hidden at the time. As Vallance comments on his website:

The difference with Tony was, he wasn't at all opposed to working with me. Some groups were dragged to my studio by their managers or record companies, kicking and screaming, not wanting to collaborate outside the band. But Tony was genuinely keen from the start, which was a nice change.

One reason the band opted for Olsen was the guitar sound he produced in the studio. Clarkin had become progressively dissatisfied with how the guitars sounded on the previous couple of albums, believing that his own demos captured the live sound of the band more accurately. As Clarkin commented to Valerie Potter in *Metal Hammer* in December 1988: 'I think the guitar does get pushed into the background'. Previous producers, he felt, had tended to think, 'Commercial, commercial! Guitar, not commercial – keyboard – commercial!' But Olsen, the band believed, had managed to capture a ballsy, gritty guitar sound, evident particularly in tracks such as 'Mama', 'Reckless Man' and 'Born To Be King'. 'This is right in your face – as they say over here', Clarkin told *Kerrang!* in June 1990, 'Everything sounds much tighter. That's what we wanted'.

Olsen also encouraged Catley to produce some particularly fine vocal performances. The singer told *Metal Hammer*'s Andy Bradshaw that Olsen 'pushed me an awful lot. He made me try things I normally wouldn't have bothered to do, gave me a lot of different ideas'. For his part, Olsen considered Catley to have 'a world-class voice' sufficient to place him 'up there with the greats, including Paul Rodgers'. He also told Bradshaw that he considered *Goodnight LA* to be 'the best album I've worked on in the last five years'.

The album had the working title, *Born To Be King*, after one of its key tracks for well over a year. The decision to name it *Goodnight LA* instead, after the studio it was recorded in, seems to have been taken quite close to the release date. The cover was designed by Hugh Syme, a renowned Canadian graphic artist most famous for his work with Rush. He had also recently been responsible for Whitesnake's *1987* and Bon Jovi's *New Jersey*. The image of an elderly gentleman riding through the sky on a unicycle differed significantly from most of the band's covers but is one of its most striking and effective.

Although the album performed creditably in the UK and throughout Europe, record company wrangles meant that it was never released in the US as intended.

'Rockin' Chair' (Clarkin and Russ Ballard) (4:10)

The opening song and first single, 'Rockin' Chair', was a sign of the gutsy, guitar-based sound that Olsen brought to the surface on the album. In a track-by-track guide for *Metal Hammer*, Clarkin described it as 'a good time track that shouldn't be taken too seriously' about a man being held back in a relationship and breaking away to have a good time. It can also be read as a tongue-in-cheek dig at the continual jibes in the rock music press at the band's age. Musically, it's one of the strongest of the guitar-heavy tracks on the album. There's certainly a clarity in the composition and a sheen in the production that makes it seem attuned to the US market at the time. But Kirk Blows' assessment in *Raw* magazine that the single was 'a calculated stab at commercialism, Americana-style, that contained not one drop of vintage Magnum character' seems more than a little unfair. Apart from anything else, it's not straightforward musically, with subtle changes aplenty throughout the track. It's also the best of the Russ Ballard co-writes.

Backed by 'Mama' on the 7" and an additional track, 'Where Do You Run To' on the 12" and CD, 'Rockin' Chair' was the last Magnum single to breach the UK Top 40. It made number 27 in June 1990 and secured another *Top Of The Pops* performance.

'Mama' (4:34)

Goodnight LA's more guitar-oriented sound is certainly evident from the first block of songs on the album and, particularly 'Mama', one of the heaviest tracks the band had produced. The slow synth and picked guitar opening are a false dawn, as at 58 seconds, the guitars crash in with riff tumbling over riff in what turns into a Clarkin masterclass. Catley's vocal is incredibly powerful throughout, demonstrating his ability to match melodic rock royalty like David Coverdale when needed. But it varies according to the requirements of different parts of the song. The words concern having someone to turn to for help when needed, someone to 'follow' and 'comfort' you. As Clarkin related, 'it could be a religious thing, a girlfriend or a mother'.

'Only A Memory' (7:04)
The album's epic is another anti-war song, this time inspired by the Falklands War. The main story arc is of a boy who has his life mapped out through school; he enters the military, where he becomes a leader – 'a beacon in the night' – but goes off to war and is killed. The 'punchline', as Clarkin put it to Valerie Potter in *Metal Hammer* in May 1989, is that for his family, he just became a memory. It's a deeply emotive track with a few poignant turns of phrase, particularly the reference to the lighting of flames as memories: 'The years of tenderness/Make them burn bright'. As a slow-moving track – the rhythm section doesn't kick in until after the first chorus at 2.24 – based on feel and mood, it does seem a little out of place among the record's direct rockers and glossy AOR cuts. But it's a lovely tune with a typically passionate Catley vocal and fabulous playing from the whole band, including space for an extended Clarkin solo towards the end.

'Reckless Man' (3:11)
The most upfront and uptempo rock song on the album, 'Reckless Man' is made for American radio, with a synth augmented guitar motif and a simple tune and message. Even here, though, there are brief intricate guitar passages and a neat keyboard solo at 1.56. A general diatribe on politicians who lie and cheat, this is a topic that Clarkin was to return to numerous times on later albums. 'Reckless Man' was the last of the triumvirate of guitar-heavy songs (with 'Rockin' Chair' and 'Mama') that was played through most of the *Goodnight LA* tour.

'Matter Of Survival' (Clarkin and Russ Ballard) (4:19)
If there's one song that does sound as if it has been written specifically for the American market, it's 'Matter Of Survival'. A ballad about a couple struggling to live together, it's a perfectly reasonable and decently performed soft rock track. Catley produces a heartfelt and sensitive performance and there's a nice saxophone solo from Deric Dyer, who had worked with Joe Cocker and Tina Turner. But the rest of the band seem to be playing within themselves on a song that simply isn't very memorable.

'What Kind Of Love Is This' (Clarkin and Jim Vallance) (4:35)
This is much better. Although it includes a synth phrase that sounds a little like Queen's 'Radio Ga Ga', it's another lively track with plenty of guitar hooks and chanted vocals. The melody, as on much of the album, is simple

but effective. It's certainly a good track, but it's difficult to see any added quality in the material written with outside writers, however talented they were.

'Heartbroke And Busted' (3:37)

The second single from the album (backed by 'Hanging Tree' with 'Cry For You' on the 12" and CD), this only made number 49 and was considered something of a failure by Polydor. Indeed, it has garnered a lot of negative comments over the years. Stanway has noted a number of times that he dislikes the song, partly because of the poor keyboard part.

However, 'Heartbroke And Busted' is actually one of the strongest songs on the record. As one of the only Magnum tracks to open with the chorus, it was clearly structured with the singles market in mind. It's rich in melody, with a verse, pre-chorus, chorus and middle eight that could all have acted as the core tune in another song. In fact, the fantastic 'And you will never know the questions you're asking' middle eight was taken from the chorus of another track the band had demoed in preparation for the album, 'Those Were The Days' (see below).

The lyrics were inspired by a beautiful woman Clarkin knew in Birmingham who had recently broken up with her husband and was feeling sorry for herself. 'I was trying', Clarkin told *Metal Hammer*, 'to push her into realising she had so many good things going for herself'.

'Shoot' (3:34)

A song detailing Clarkin's thoughts about terrorism and about the killing of innocent people, 'Shoot' isn't the most sophisticated of lyrics. Neither does the subject matter easily fit with the fairly light temper of the music. The melody is solid and there are some cleverly placed backing vocals, but ultimately, this is one of *Goodnight LA*'s lesser tracks.

'No Way Out' (Clarkin and Russ Ballard) (3:59)

This is the third Clarkin/Ballard composition on the album and was intended as the third single before Polydor pulled the plug after 'Heartbroke And Busted' had flopped. Inspired by the experiences of illegal immigrants in the United States, it's another solid track given an AOR gloss by Olsen's production. The main riff is pure melodic rock heaven and the song could easily have become a European or even US hit single if released a few years earlier.

'Cry For You' (Clarkin and Sue Shifrin) (3:57)

A fairly routine ballad, 'Cry For You' is one of the *Goodnight LA* tracks that seems just a stretch too far from the band's established sound. There's nothing wrong with it in itself, but in the context of a Magnum album, it just appears tepid and soulless. Perhaps the band themselves were unsure about it as it wasn't included on the vinyl or cassette versions of the album.

'Born To Be King' (5:33)

Despite the album's uneven quality, *Goodnight LA* finishes with a classic Magnum track on a par with the best barnstormers of the previous decade, like 'Soldier Of The Line' and 'Vigilante'. It's blessed with a tricksy guitar riff that clears the way for the inventive truncated vocal lines that mirror the syncopated rhythm. The main instrumentation breaks down at 2.34 into an ambient section with some lovely subtle percussion that, at 3.29, ramps up into repeated chants of 'He was born to be king'. The furious finale, from 3.50 onwards, is one of the most riveting instrumental sections that the band have committed to vinyl, with Clarkin, Lowe and Barker, especially, in imperious form.

Although somewhat circumspect in earlier interviews, by the time of the album's release, Clarkin was unequivocal about the meaning of the song. As he told *Metal Hammer*:

'Born To Be King' is about Jesus Christ, who was born to be king. I'm a Christian and always have been, although I don't like to ram it down people's throats. It's just something that I am and something I feel happy with.

Related Tracks
'Where Do You Run To' (3:44)

The existence of the next two songs on the B-sides and 12" formats of the *Goodnight LA* singles is indicative of the skewed process of song selection for the album. Both are top-drawer Clarkin compositions that may have been regarded as too close to the familiar Magnum sound to make the cut. Produced by Magnum and Saga keyboardist Jim Crichton (misspelt on the sleeve), 'Where Do You Run To' (they also seemed afraid of question marks) featured on the 12" and CD single of 'Rockin' Chair'. It's a dynamic, uplifting track with plenty of melodic touches held together by a fine ensemble performance.

'Hanging Tree' (3:37)

The B-side to 'Heartbroke And Busted', 'Hanging Tree' (also produced by the band rather than Olsen) would not only have been worthy of inclusion but would have been one of the best songs on *Goodnight LA*. Driven by an insanely catchy riff, which Catley's vocals echo towards the end of the song, there's more energy here than on most of the AOR-leaning tunes on the album put together. A song about the Ku Klux Klan, it was inspired by Billie Holliday's famous 1939 song, 'Strange Fruit', which tells of the lynching of Black Americans in the southern states.

'Those Were The Days' (4:12)

Included as an extra track on the 2CD edition of *On The Thirteenth Day* in 2012, 'Those Were The Days' is a demo from 1988-89. It was mentioned as one of the earliest songs worked up by the band in magazine features in December 1988; writing in *Kerrang!*, Lyn Guy described it as a 'potential chart smash'. It's a pleasant, laid-back tune, but its similarity to 'Days Of No Trust' might have dissuaded the band from developing it further. The chorus, as noted above, was pilfered for the middle eight of 'Heartbroke And Busted'.

Sleepwalking (1992)

Personnel:
Tony Clarkin: guitar and vocals
Bob Catley: lead vocals
Mark Stanway: keyboards
Wally Lowe: bass guitar and vocals
Mickey Barker: drums
Additional musicians:
Wesley Magoogan: saxophone on 'Every Woman, Every Man' and 'The Long Ride'
Pritam Singh: tablas on 'Prayer For A Stranger'
Gary Sanders: harmonica on 'The Long Ride'
York Gibson: keyboard programming
Produced at Zella Studios, Birmingham by Tony Clarkin
Engineer: York Gibson
Assistant Engineer: Mike Cowling
Release date: 12 October 1992 on Music for Nations
Cover Design: Rodney Matthews
Highest chart places: UK: 27, Germany: 67, Sweden: 29
Running time: 52:56

Much had changed for Magnum by the time the band reconvened for the recording sessions for the follow-up to *Goodnight LA* in 1991. Dissatisfied with the record company's failure to adequately promote the band, they left Polydor. A number of factors seem to have prompted the decision. On top of Polydor's rejection of Rodney Matthews' artwork for *Goodnight LA*, the band were frustrated by the label's lack of interest in 1991's *The Spirit* live album: 'We felt the album needed to come out as quickly as possible', Clarkin recalled, 'yet we knew that Polydor wouldn't put anything behind it'.

The band had to pay to leave the label, but they were sure it was the right move: 'There's no point in being with a big label if they don't understand the band'. A deal was soon struck with independent label Music For Nations, who agreed to make Magnum's next album a priority release.

At the same time, the band decided to self-produce for the first time since 1983's *The Eleventh Hour*. Clarkin thought he had acquired sufficient knowledge and ideas from the producers the band had worked with in the previous decade to do the job himself again. For his part, Catley told *Kerrang!* that Clarkin knew better than anyone else 'what Magnum should sound like'.

The album was recorded at Magnum's own Zella Studios in Birmingham. This allowed the band to take more time over recording; six months rather than the usual three. According to Clarkin: 'This gave us more time to concentrate on what we wanted to do... It gave us a lot more time to concentrate on the music ... on getting the right feel for everybody's playing'.

Drummer Mickey Barker remembered *Sleepwalking* as the album where the band took back control and thought it a better record as a result. For Clarkin, it sounded like a band playing together again. He believed that his own laid-back production (he described it to *Kerrang!* as 'an *un*-produced album') provided a live, raw and exciting sound that set it apart from recent releases.

For all these attempts to distance *Sleepwalking* from *Goodnight LA*, there's a great deal of continuity between the two albums. Taken together, they're the most explicitly commercial records in the Magnum catalogue. The AOR vibe that came to the fore on some of the *Goodnight LA* material is similarly evident across a good proportion of *Sleepwalking*, particularly on songs such as 'Too Much To Ask', 'You're The One' and 'Just One More Heartbreak'. But there's also a new-found diversity in the band's sound, with the introduction, in particular, of blues and Americana influences as well as the addition of harmonica and even tabla, alongside the more liberal use of saxophone, to Magnum's more or less traditional hard rock instrumentation.

The artwork saw the return of Rodney Matthews, his first Magnum cover since *On A Storyteller's Night*. Eschewing his usual fantasy approach, Matthews' illustration of a magical bedroom is cluttered with references to the album's songs and previous covers. The flag-waving Jack-in-a-Box ('Only In America'), native American head-dress ('The Flood'), storm clouds ('Stormy Weather') and the number one on the wall behind the bed ('You're The One') are the most obvious references to the album content. The 'ghost in the mirror' and red shoes under the bed reference lyrics in the title track. Elsewhere, the dragon from *Chase The Dragon* sits on the windowsill, *The Spirit* cover adorns the bedroom mat, *The Eleventh Hour* jets are on the wall, the stick, sack and mice from *On A Storyteller's Night* appear on the left of the image and *Wings Of Heaven*, *Magnum II* and *Kingdom Of Madness* LPs are scattered across the floor. Matthews also designed a new Magnum logo, possibly to fit with the cartoonish style of the cover illustration.

The title of the album changed a number of times. Originally *Sleepwalking*, it was altered to *Nightwatch* to avoid confusion with Stephen King's upcoming *Sleepwalkers* film. The band then reverted to the original title after Clarkin had done some editing on the track 'Sleepwalking', which meant it would be included on the album after all.

'Stormy Weather' (4:42)
The album begins with one of Magnum's most atmospheric and emotive tracks. Influenced by the landscape of coastal Devon in southwest England, where Clarkin was living at the time, the lyrics make a straightforward but effective comparison between meteorology and relationships. As he told *Kerrang!*'s Dave Reynolds: 'these lonely, dark, stormy nights... just felt like the break-up of a long-term relationship'.

'Stormy Weather' may be an unconventional choice to open the album, but it works well. The song's lilting, reflective mood underlines a depth to

Above: The five members of Magnum's 'classic' line-up during the filming of the 'Rockin' Chair' video in June 1990. (*Alamy*)

Left: The UK cover of *Kingdom Of Madness*, the eclectic debut album from 1978 that mixed progressive, hard rock and melodic sounds (as well as a hint of disco). (*Jet*)

Right: The second album, *Magnum II*, disappointed critics but represented a step forward in song quality and performance. (*Jet*)

Left: The first of Rodney Matthews' iconic Magnum sleeve designs was originally intended as a gatefold sleeve. Charting in the UK at number 17, *Chase The Dragon* contains some of the band's most enduring songs. (*Jet*)

Right: *The Eleventh Hour* from 1983 is often dismissed as being poorly produced, with over-complicated song structures, but is actually among the strongest of the band's early work. (*Jet*)

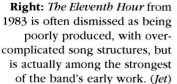

Left: *On A Storyteller's Night* from 1985 is the album that saved the band and won them a contract with Polydor, adorned with one of the greatest fantasy sleeves of all time. (*FM*)

Right: Recorded at Queen's Montreux Studios in Switzerland, *Vigilante* is shaped by characteristically 1980s production but has a raft of great songs. (*Polydor*)

Left: The high point of the band's commercial success, *Wings Of Heaven* reached number five in the UK album charts in 1988. (*Polydor*)

Right: Named after the Los Angeles studio where it was recorded, 1990's *Goodnight LA* provoked a backlash among some music journalists who thought the band had gone too commercial. (*Polydor*)

Left: Rodney Matthews' *Sleepwalking* design, his first sleeve for seven years, is full of in-jokes and references to previous albums. (*Music For Nations*)

Right: Magnum hitched onto the 'unplugged' craze of the 1990s with *Keeping The Nite Light Burning*, a stripped-back treatment of classic songs. (*Jet*)

Left: *Rock Art* was the final album recorded by the successful 1980s line-up and the last before the band split up in 1995. (*EMI*)

Right: *Breath Of Life*, the reunion album, has its moments but is not among the band's best efforts. (*SPV*)

Left: The 1984 Spring tour featured the final live appearances of drummer Kex Gorin and the first outing of songs from what was to become the *On A Storyteller's Night* album. (*Author's Collection*)

Right: The programme from the 1990 *Goodnight LA* tour, which took the band to Birmingham's NEC and Wembley Arena. (*Author's Collection*)

Right: Magnum were well-supported by the rock press during the 1980s and featured frequently on the cover of the UK's *Kerrang!* magazine. (*Kerrang!/Author's Collection*)

Left: Another magazine feature detailing the band's exploits in Los Angeles recording the *Goodnight LA* album. (*Metal Hammer/ Author's Collection*)

Left: A still from the futuristic 'Days Of No Trust' video, with Tony Clarkin wearing his trademark hat.

Right: A shot from the Christmas 1992 Birmingham Town Hall concert that featured on the DVD releases *A Winter's Tale* and *Live At Birmingham*.

Left: Bob Catley and Tony Clarkin (minus hat and hair) during the Christmas 1992 concert.

Right: *Brand New Morning* was a return to form that showcased a harder-edged sound. (*SPV*)

Left: One of the most popular albums of the reunion phase, 2007's *Princess Alice And The Broken Arrow* signalled the return of the fantasy artwork of Rodney Matthews. (*SPV*)

Right: The cover of *Into The Valley Of The Moonking* from 2009 introduced the character of the schoolboy, who went on to feature on a number of later album sleeves. (*SPV*)

Left: *The Visitation* features one of Rodney Matthews' more unusual cover designs, again with numerous visual references to earlier songs, albums and sleeves. (*SPV*)

Right: *On The Thirteenth Day* is possibly the most diverse and accomplished Magnum album of the 21st century, though the cover art is a little disappointing. (*SPV*)

Left: *Escape From The Shadow Garden* from 2014 boasts another striking fantasy sleeve and the return of the *On A Storyteller's Night* logo. (*SPV*)

Right: The final album with keyboardist Mark Stanway and drummer Harry James, the music and cover art of *Sacred Blood 'Divine' Lies* reflect a band running a little out of ideas. (*SPV*)

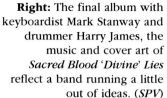

Left: One of Rodney Matthews' favourite cover designs adorns *Lost On The Road To Eternity*, on which the band sound re-energised. (*SPV*)

Right: 2020's *The Serpent Rings* includes a host of progressive musical and lyrical ideas and a first-class fantasy sleeve. (*SPV*)

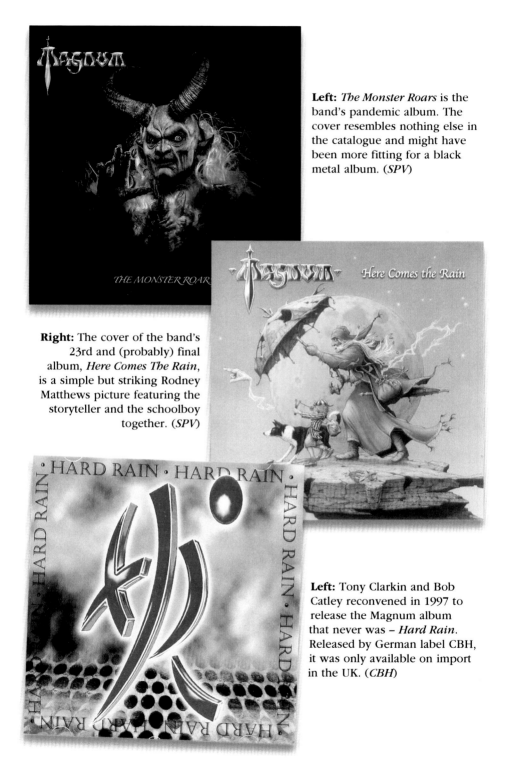

Left: *The Monster Roars* is the band's pandemic album. The cover resembles nothing else in the catalogue and might have been more fitting for a black metal album. (*SPV*)

Right: The cover of the band's 23rd and (probably) final album, *Here Comes The Rain*, is a simple but striking Rodney Matthews picture featuring the storyteller and the schoolboy together. (*SPV*)

Left: Tony Clarkin and Bob Catley reconvened in 1997 to release the Magnum album that never was – *Hard Rain*. Released by German label CBH, it was only available on import in the UK. (*CBH*)

Right: *Marauder* from 1980 is the first Magnum live album. Its generic sleeve may have been partly responsible for the common misrepresentation of Magnum as a heavy metal band. (*Jet*)

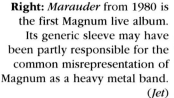

Left: Originally intended as a double live album, *The Spirit* ended up as the band's final release on Polydor Records. (*Polydor*)

Right: *Escape From The Shadow Garden Live 2014* showcases a heavier guitar-dominated sound that the band had been developing across a number of albums. (*SPV*)

Left: Magnum performing at the High Voltage Festival in London in 2010.

Right: Charismatic bassist Al Barrow on stage with Bob Catley. Barrow has been an essential part of the Magnum 'family' since joining the band in 2001.

Left: Tony Clarkin onstage in 2010. An underrated musician, Clarkin eschewed extended soloing that didn't serve the song.

Right: Bob Catley, the voice and heart of Magnum, onstage. Producer Keith Olsen considered Catley to have 'a world-class voice' that was 'up there with the best'.

Left: A live shot of Harry James, who was in the band from 2002-2005 and 2007-2017. For most of that period, he was also the drummer for Thunder.

Right: The band's reputation as an impressive live act, established in the 1980s, was sustained by consistent touring during the reunion phase.

Left: The line-up for the second Hard Rain album, *When The Good Times Come,* included Al Barrow, later a permanent member of Magnum, and Sue McCloskey, who co-wrote two tracks on *Breath Of Life. (Eagle)*

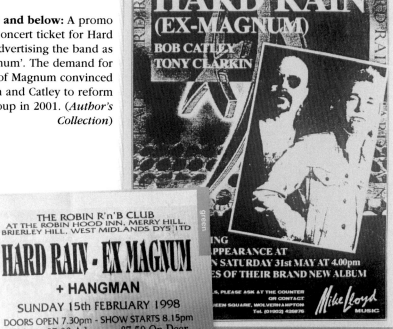

Right and below: A promo flyer and concert ticket for Hard Rain advertising the band as 'ex-Magnum'. The demand for the return of Magnum convinced Clarkin and Catley to reform the group in 2001. (*Author's Collection*)

Clarkin's songwriting that is perhaps less evident in the more commercial cuts that follow. It's underpinned by a slow and funky Lowe bass line, which meshes perfectly with Barker's sensitive drumming. Clarkin's lovely guitar phrases help to lift the song while Catley puts in an emotional vocal performance on par with his best work on *Goodnight LA*.

'Stormy Weather' is Magnum at their heartfelt and expressive best. Given the undoubted quality of the song, it's surprising that the band only chose to play it intermittently on tour, although it did feature at the 1992 Christmas homecoming show at Birmingham Town Hall.

'Too Much To Ask' (5:00)
This is a well-structured hard rock track with a light, commercial edge. It is built on a robust riff reminiscent of Deep Purple with a chorus that moves it into pure AOR territory. It may be slightly overlong, but it's as good as anything on contemporaneous albums by melodic rock titans such as Def Leppard and Europe. The band seem comfortable in their own skin here in a way that they didn't on some of the weaker co-written *Goodnight LA* tracks.

'You're The One' (3:45)
The best of the AOR-ish tracks on *Sleepwalking*, 'You're The One' is a Top 20 single in waiting. It was in fact, intended as the album's second single, but the poor performance of 'Only In America' meant it was never released. It may not have sold any better, but 'You're The One' is a more immediate track with greater crossover potential to the UK singles market. Ironically, for a title suggesting straightforward romantic attraction, the song recounts the end of a relationship: 'You're the one, you're the one who walked out on me/You're the one, you're the one who'll be history'. The version played live throughout the *Sleepwalking* tour included a jazzy Stanway keyboard break and some especially energetic drumming from Barker.

'The Flood (Red Cloud's War)' (6:03)
Like 'Stormy Weather', 'The Flood' is a delicate and brooding masterpiece that stands out among the more conventional melodic rock tunes on *Sleepwalking*. Built on a rich keyboard arrangement and simple but effective guitar chords, this is a song elevated by fine ensemble playing and subtle switches in dynamics. It's another affecting vocal performance, with dramatic moments such as Catley's soaring voice on the 'You got talked out of dreams' line. But the real star of the show here is Barker, whose drum fills at around 3.10-3.24 and 4.35-4.50 are simply awe-inspiring. The extended ending involving some fine Clarkin soloing that then drops into Barker's drum roll finale is one of the band's best.

The lyrics are influenced by the American historian Dee Brown's groundbreaking 1970 book, *Bury My Heart At Wounded Knee*, a critical account of government expansion into the American West in the late 19th century, the displacement and forced relocation of Native Americans and the destruction of their culture. The song's subtitle references the 1866-68 armed conflict between an alliance of the Lakota, Northern Cheyenne and Northern Arapaho peoples and the US government over the Powder River Country in Wyoming and Montana. Red Cloud was the name of one of the most important Lakota leaders who played a key role in the conflict. The subject matter is reflected in the wordless backing vocals in the chorus and the flute-like synth embellishments in the first verse that seem to echo aspects of Native American music.

'Broken Wheel' (3:59)
We're in fairly standard ballad territory – musically and lyrically – for this song. The introduction is a dead-ringer for a slowed-down 'Days Of No Trust' and, more generally, this is a track that harks back to the *Wings Of Heaven* era, particularly some of the excellent B-sides. Laid-back and piano/keyboard-led, with some interesting guitar embellishment, it's a good addition to Magnum's catalogue of ballads, even if the chorus doesn't really take the song anywhere and the lyrics are pretty uninspired. The re-recorded *Valley Of Tears* version adds some heft to the guitar and drum sound, but otherwise, there's little difference.

'Just One More Heartbreak' (4:10)
Along with 'Broken Wheel', this was featured on the 1991 *The Spirit* tour under the title, 'Turn Me Loose'. It's a well-written pop-metal tune with some nice hooks. But it's marred by dated 1980s synth effects reminiscent of some of Def Leppard's excessively-programmed arrangements. With more sensitive production, this might have been transformed into a hard-edged rock track similar to *Goodnight LA*'s 'Reckless Man'. The band sound like they're having a good time, but it's one of the least effective of the album's more commercial tracks.

'Every Woman, Every Man' (4:07)
Clarkin's love of Bruce Springsteen shines through in this sun-drenched track. The first Magnum song to utilise saxophone for the main melodic hook, 'Every Woman, Every Man' is a real grower that shows off the power and range of Catley's lead vocals and includes some inspired backing vocals in the chorus. The song is held down by Lowe's insistent bass line and precision drumming from Barker. It may be a little outside Magnum's comfort zone but it demonstrates the versatility of both Clarkin's writing and the musicianship of what was, by now, a very experienced band.

'Only In America' (4:01)
An unusually funky song by Magnum standards, with a powerful singalong chorus, 'Only In America' was singled out by reviewers and was a favourite

of many around the band, including cover artist Rodney Matthews. The lyrics are based on a diary kept by Clarkin of the things he had observed while in the States. Although there are one or two clever couplets – 'Pay to play/ work for food', which juxtaposes the exploitation of rock bands with severe poverty, for example – the subject matter is actually rather hackneyed. Given the criticism in some quarters that the band had gone 'too American' on the previous album, it was also perhaps a mistake for the next single to be focused on that American experience.

'Only In America' b/w 'Sleepwalking' was released on 5 October 1992. An edited version of the A-side was included on the 7" disc. It was the first single for ten years – since 1982's 'Live In America' EP – to fail to reach the Top 100 in the UK charts.

'Sleepwalking' (5:39)

The title track is one of the more complex and varied compositions on the album. It's based on a sinuous guitar riff that blends into a driving keyboard refrain. The verse is upbeat and poppy, but it's on the bridge and chorus (where the guitar and keyboard riffs repeat) that the song really takes off. There's a lovely acoustic interlude from 2.37 that builds back into the main riff at 4.10. The final twist is a short bluesy coda that fades out before it has got going.

According to Martin Vielhaber's online biography, 'Sleepwalking' is an autobiographical track reflecting on some of Clarkin's life experiences, such as the end of the Cold War. There's certainly a host of interesting literary and cultural references to *The Wizard Of Oz*, Richard Bach's novella, *Jonathan Livingston Seagull* and J. D. Salinger's *Catcher In The Rye* (with a possible nod to the 1980 murder of John Lennon), for instance. But the precise meaning of the song is rather elusive.

The song featured throughout the accompanying tour but soon disappeared from the setlist along with most of the *Sleepwalking* tracks.

'Prayer For A Stranger' (4:21)

A light break between two of the album's longer and more substantial songs, this track is neither catchy nor distinctive enough to leave a significant impression. It's arguably more pop than rock and suffers from irritating vocal effects. The inclusion of some gorgeous tabla playing from Pritam Singh – and a middle eight, which is considerably better than the rest of the song – doesn't quite save it.

'The Long Ride' (6:55)

The album closes with this slow-moving, soulful tune cut from a similar cloth as *Wings Of Heaven*'s 'One Step Away'. Based around a standard blues structure, it's unusual in the Magnum catalogue to allow space for instrumental exploration. Alongside some nice guitar licks, Wesley Magoogan's saxophone is again prominent and Gary Sanders' bursts of harmonica (oddly reminiscent of the harmonica/melodica playing on The The's 1989 *Mindbomb* album) give the song a fairly loose (by Magnum standards), almost sludgy vibe. Catley's versatility is again on display, particularly in the low register, almost spoken word verses. The final minute and a half is fabulously chaotic and about the closest the band have come to a full-scale jam on a studio recording.

Related Tracks
'Just A Little Bit' (3:59)
The two additional tracks on the 'Only In America' 12" and CD single are both straight-down-the-line AOR. 'Just A Little Bit' is a well-crafted, upbeat tune made for American radio. It's about as pop rock as Magnum ever got, with a sound closer to Bryan Adams than Def Leppard or Whitesnake. It's an enjoyable four minutes, but you do get the feeling that Clarkin could write this type of song in his sleep.

'Caught In Love' (3:50)
This is in a similar soft rock vein, with a catchy strummed guitar refrain and a singalong chorus. There are one or two signature Magnum atmospheric passages, but they're soon swept away by the repeated melody lines. 'Caught In Love' was set for inclusion on the album until Clarkin reworked the title track, which eventually replaced it. It works better as a bonus track and would have shifted the balance of the album too much towards AOR.

Keeping The Nite Light Burning (1993)

Personnel:
The Nite Lighters:
Tony Clarkin: acoustic and slide guitars and vocals
Bob Catley: vocals and tambourine
Mark Stanway: grand piano and electric piano
Wally Lowe: bass guitar and vocals
Mickey Barker: drums, hand drums and percussion
Additional musicians:
The Red Lemon Horns:
Paul Roberts: trombone
Bob Poutney: trumpet
Rob Hughes: saxophone
Gill Stevenson: cello
Produced at Magnum Studios, Birmingham, by Tony Clarkin
Engineer: Mike Cowling
Release date: 15 November 1993 on Jet Records
Cover Photograph: Simon Harding Photography
Highest chart places: UK, Germany and Sweden: Did Not Chart
Running time: 48:43

This decision to record an acoustic album needs to be seen in the context of a period when the MTV unplugged phenomenon was at its height. Magnum had previously dabbled with acoustic recordings, most successfully with the lovely version of 'Les Morts Dansant' that appeared on the 'Heartbroke And Busted' four-track EP in 1990. The intention had originally been to revisit a number of the band's earlier recordings with minimal instrumentation – just acoustic guitar, vocals and bass – but that soon snowballed into more complex arrangements involving the whole band as well as a horn section and cello. What had been intended as a two-week project took around two and a half months to complete.

The album's liner notes describe the appeal of 'giving some old favourites "new suits" unrestricted by style and form besides those naturally associated with the word "acoustic"'. In an interview from 1993 included in the *On A Storyteller's Night* expanded edition, Clarkin noted how proud they were of the album, considering it 'very different to anything we've ever done' but feeling that they'd learnt a lot that would help them with future recordings. Catley, meanwhile, has said in a number of interviews that *Keeping The Nite Light Burning* may be his favourite Magnum record. It was produced by Clarkin at the band's own studio, now renamed Magnum Studios.

Keeping The Nite Light Burning is a worthwhile album that warrants a place in the band's discography. Opting for a range of styles across the record rather than a consistent approach was risky as there were bound to be some that were less successful than others. So, too, was the decision to pick only one song from the band's best-selling albums, *On A Storyteller's Night* and *Wings Of Heaven*. Despite this, the album contains a handful of excellent, innovative recordings and even the experiments that didn't quite pay off are at least interesting. The cover was a simple affair with a black and white photograph of the band and Matthews' newest logo from *Sleepwalking* in blue neon.

Magnum promoted the upcoming album in the spring of 1993 by including acoustic slots within their conventional electric shows. This was continued at certain live dates through the remainder of the year and into 1994.

'The Prize' (4:41) (Original version on *The Eleventh Hour*, 1983)
The album begins with this lovely arrangement of one of the band's classic tunes. Cello and acoustic guitar provide the song with a solemn atmosphere while the 6/8 time signature (changed from the original 4/4) affords it a lilting, waltz-like quality. Lowe's deep bass line also operates nicely in unison with the guitar and cello. The instrumentation builds up slowly with added percussion and then eases off for the final section. The harmonised vocals are an added treat.

'Heart Broken Busted' (3:32) (Original version on *Goodnight LA*, 1990)
This is a much more conventional, pared-down interpretation of the band's last charting single. Stanway's piano part provides a sturdy backbone to some lovely acoustic and slide guitar work. As with much of the album, trimming the song down to its bare bones reveals its quality. It's unclear whether the slight title change was a printing mistake or a conscious decision.

'Foolish Heart' (2:57) (Original version on *Magnum II*, 1979)
The Red Lemon Horns take centre stage for this spirited rendition of another of the band's singles. It works well enough in this guise. The saxophone solo is particularly impressive and Catley's vocal is, in parts, awe-inspiring. It's especially impressive on what seems to be a newly composed bridge between 1.43-1.58. Yet, in truth, the sound is so different that it's unlikely many Magnum fans would have played this after the first listen.

'Lonely Nights' (4:18) (Original version on *Vigilante*, 1986)
In view of the sterile, somewhat processed character of the original, this is a track crying out for a more organic treatment. It's reimagined here as a meditative ballad, more in line, one could argue, with the lyrical content. As well as fine melancholic backing vocals, this boasts excellent acoustic guitar and piano solos. A re-recorded version of the same basic arrangement – but with synths and an electric rather than an acoustic guitar break – was included on *The Valley Of Tears – The Ballads* compilation in 2017.

'Start Talking Love' (3:41) (Original version on *Wings Of Heaven*, 1988)
Magnum's most successful single is given a simple, upbeat acoustic treatment, with some interesting rhythmic variation. Barker's percussion plays a big

part. There are imaginative touches here and there but the core of the song remains intact and not too dissimilar from the original arrangement.

'Only A Memory' (3:44) (Original version on *Goodnight LA*, 1990)
This is an entirely acapella rendition of one of the best tunes on *Goodnight LA*. The first 20 seconds are Catley's naked vocal, but thereafter, the musical backing is provided by a multi-tracked layering of solemn choral voices. It's a wonderfully effective arrangement that brings out the brittle emotion of the lyric.

'Need A Lot Of Love' (5:42) (Original version on *Vigilante*, 1986)
This is a full-on reggae interpretation of one of the band's more commercial singles. There are a number of nice moments here, including some imaginative cello interventions from Gill Stevenson. Above all, the track clearly brings out the versatility and quality of Lowe's driving bass playing and Barker's precise percussion. Nonetheless, it's an impressive rather than a particularly pleasurable listen. The arrangement is a little awkward in places and it seriously drags towards the end.

'Maybe Tonight' (3:30) (Original version, B-Side of 'Days Of No Trust', 1988)
This is further evidence, if it were needed, of the quality of a song that, let's not forget, was originally only a B-side. With one of the most straightforward arrangements on the album, focusing especially on guitar and piano, the band transform 'Maybe Tonight' from a feel-good rocker into a laid-back ballad. It's a beautifully simple rendition, topped off by Catley's sensitive handling of the vocals.

'One Night Of Passion' (3:53) (Original version on *The Eleventh Hour*, 1983)
If there's a song in the Magnum catalogue that's apt for this type of jazzy interpretation, it's 'One Night Of Passion'. It's great to hear Lowe's intricate bass work as high in the mix as it is here. Clarkin's acoustic meanderings are also inspired, lifting what's otherwise only a fair arrangement of one of the band's weaker songs.

'Without Your Love' (4:46) (Original version from *Kingdom Of Madness* sessions, released on *Archive*, 1993)
This is a rich, soulful version of the oldest track on the album. It's worth remembering that with the *Archive* collection having just been released, 'Without Your Love' would only have been known by the most ardent Magnum fans at the time. It's a great rendition. Acoustic and slide guitars and piano blend seamlessly and Catley's mature vocal brings an emotional depth that the original doesn't really come close to.

'Shoot' (4:00) (Original version on *Goodnight LA*, 1990)
One of the less radical adaptations on the album, this straightforward acoustic rendering strips the song of much of its excessive studio gloss. While that may be sufficient to argue that it's a better version than the *Goodnight LA* track, it doesn't make it one of the standout tracks on this album.

'Soldier Of The Line' (3:59) (Original version on *Chase The Dragon*, 1982)
Although it can be dangerous to mess with the most popular tracks, Magnum get it right with this stunningly constructed, dark and atmospheric interpretation of 'Soldier Of The Line'. The instrumentation shifts throughout the song's four minutes, from a solo piano in the first verse to a rumbling bass-heavy chorus that then morphs into a cello and acoustic guitar section. It all holds together well, possibly because the band maintain a hard rock sensibility on this final track that is sidelined elsewhere on the record.

Rock Art (1994)

Personnel:
Tony Clarkin: guitars and vocals
Bob Catley: vocals
Mark Stanway: keyboards
Wally Lowe: bass guitar and vocals
Mickey Barker: drums and percussion
Additional musicians:
Jacki Graham: backing vocals
Mo Birch: backing vocals
P. J. Wright: pedal steel guitars
Produced at Magnum Studios, Birmingham by Tony Clarkin
Engineer: Stephen Harris
Second Engineer: Mike Cowling
Release date: 6 June 1994 on EMI Germany
Cover Artwork: Eleanor Smith
Highest chart places: UK: 57, Germany: 83, Sweden: 24
Running time: 55:00

Magnum's 11th album arrived at a time of immense change in the musical landscape, a few years after the emergence of grunge and at the height of Britpop. Never a band connected to the zeitgeist at the best of times, Magnum seemed out of step with musical trends as never before. Although a core fanbase remained, the records were selling less and the concert venues became smaller.

Because of this, and the fact that it was the last album before the break-up of the band in 1995, *Rock Art* has tended to be regarded as a career low-point. There's certainly some weak material on the album, but it also includes a couple of Clarkin's very best compositions and is as varied a record as the band has ever produced. In retrospect, it can be regarded as a solid ending to the band's first phase and a record that stands up well alongside the other perennially underrated 1990s albums that preceded it.

The album came together in late 1993, as the band demoed a number of songs that were already featured in the live set – 'Hard Hearted Woman', 'Rock Heavy' and 'On Christmas Day' – as well as a new ballad, 'Back In Your Arms Again'. Another track, 'Hush-A-Bye-Baby', seems to have existed in demo form as early as 1988.

Rock Art was the third album in a row recorded at the band's own studio in Birmingham and Clarkin produced again. It was engineered by Stephen Harris, who went on to work with Kula Shaker, the Dave Matthews Band and Kaiser Chiefs, among others. A number of members recall the sessions particularly fondly. Stanway told *Kerrang!* at the time that he hadn't 'had as much freedom making a Magnum record in 14 years with the band. It was a totally pleasurable experience and the sense of enthusiasm was relentless'.

It was a time, he later remembered, when all members had an input into the recording and the songs were 'thrashed out' together as a band.

For Clarkin, the album also represented freedom from interfering managers and record companies 'coming in and telling us what we should sound like'. It seemed, to Clarkin, 'a bit like being reborn'. '[W]e had started to get it right', he told Dave Ling in 2022, 'just about everything was right with that album. It had some really great songs'.

Originally planned to be released in spring 1994 with the German arm of EMI records, it was then delayed until the summer. This meant that the first leg of the tour in April and May in the UK included at least six songs unfamiliar to the crowd. The band's confidence in the album was evident in the fact that seven or eight of the tracks were regularly included in the tour setlist.

The album is named after Stone Age cave paintings that Clarkin had seen either in a book or in a documentary. The cover is probably the best of the band's non-Rodney Matthews designs. Put together by artist Eleanor Smith, it shows a Native American chief in headdress and war paint against a colourful patterned background dominated by yellows, oranges, browns and blues. The 'art' pun was extended to the framed portraits of band members in the inner sleeve. Chris Moore's *Vigilante* logo was also revived with some modifications, as the M's were extended at either end.

'We All Need To Be Loved' (5:05)
Long-term fans listening to the record for the first time may have been comforted by the familiar sound of the opening track. This is a full-blooded, fast-paced song in a recognisable Magnum style augmented, in particular, by thunderous drumming from Barker and an intricate Lowe bass line. The song's five minutes don't drag. There's a relentless energy and a constant shifting between the song's four discrete sections, most of which boast great hooks. There's a decent acoustic version included as a bonus track on 2002's *Breath Of Life*. But it's the sheer vigour and over-blown splendour of the original that mark it out as one of Magnum's forgotten classics.

'Hard Hearted Woman' (3:49)
The first of *Rock Art*'s genre experiments, 'Hard Hearted Woman' is a serviceable pastiche of early Whitesnake. This was probably one of the tracks on which the band felt free to play fast and loose. But in truth, it's a bit of a let-down after such a high-quality opening to the album. The vocal performance is solid and the playing is spot on, but there are no surprises here and the characteristic Magnum sound has been dispensed with.

'Back In Your Arms Again' (5:59)
If Clarkin had already established himself as one of hard rock's best ballad writers during the 1980s, 'Back In Your Arms Again' was the track which

refined the formula and provided a model that the band followed closely during its post-reformation phase. It encapsulates many of the elements that the music historian David Metzer has defined as characteristic of power ballads from the 1970s onwards. This includes a musical escalation from a quiet, minimalist opening to fuller and more dynamic instrumentation; a combination of sentimentality and uplift that provides 'both wringing sorrow and stirring music'; and a climactic guitar solo offering 'release and transcendence'. Although, not surprisingly, Magnum are ignored in Metzer's analysis, Clarkin has arguably been one of the most significant composers of this type of emotionally expressive rock music in Europe, at least, since the 1970s.

In many respects, 'Back In Your Arms Again' is the archetypal Magnum ballad. The song begins with Catley delivering an impassioned yet delicate vocal over a bedrock of chiming piano and single-note synth backing. Drums and bass are introduced in the second verse and power chords and vocal harmonies come crashing in for the chorus. The middle eight leads into a typically moving but concise Clarkin guitar solo. In common with a number of his ballads, rather than increasing the intensity to the finale, Clarkin pulls things back to the original instrumentation at around 4:30 and builds up again slowly with some inventive guitar and vocal noodling around the main melody. It's formulaic, certainly, but also characteristic of a particular Magnum take on the rock ballad that Clarkin was in the process of perfecting.

'Back In Your Arms Again' was the second single released from the album but in continental Europe only and only on CD. The song was re-recorded with the then-current line-up for 2017's *The Valley Of Tears* compilation, but aside from a slightly brighter overall sound, there's little difference.

'Rock Heavy' (3:58)
Another stylistic experiment, 'Rock Heavy' combines heavy guitars with a reggae-flavoured rhythmic accompaniment. The reggae influence isn't as surprising as it might first seem, given the prominence of that style of music in the band's hometown of Birmingham and the success of Birmingham groups such as Steel Pulse and UB40, whose recording studio Magnum had, of course, hired for *On A Storyteller's Night*. The band had already recorded a reggae-infused version of 'Need A Lot Of Love' on the previous year's *Keeping The Nite Light Burning*.

In spite of this, 'Rock Heavy' comes across as a heavy-handed attempt to fuse hard rock and reggae. It isn't helped by having one of the album's weaker melody lines and lyrics that are well below Clarkin's usual standard.

'The Tall Ships' (5:06)
Next up is *Rock Art*'s most celebrated track and for good reason. Clarkin's tale of a clipper travelling from Europe to South America around the turn of the 20th century creates an atmosphere of tranquillity that is also deeply moving

and evocative. The honey-soaked melody in the chorus floats beautifully on the rhythmic foundation provided by Barker and Lowe, as well as Stanway's insistent keyboard parp. P. J. Wright's pedal steel adds an extra dimension to the song, reinforcing the wistful mood that chimes so well with intimations of separation and emotional longing in the lyrics.

The first single from the album, 'The Tall Ships' was regularly included in the concert setlist during the final two years of Magnum's original incarnation. It remains a favourite of many former members of the band. Speaking to Mark Dean in 2012, Stanway singled out 'The Tall Ships' as among 'the best songs that Tony has ever written'. It is also a track that has been regularly included in the setlist of Kingdom of Madness, the band Stanway formed with other former members to play 'classic era' Magnum songs subsequent to leaving Magnum in 2016.

'Tell Tale Eyes' (4:52)
The best of the album's more straightforward rock tracks, 'Tell Tale Eyes' includes a number of heavy, memorable riffs. It begins sounding like a NWOBHM track before morphing into a blues rock style, again reminiscent of Bernie Marsden-era Whitesnake. Lyrically, it's disappointing, conforming to sub-par Coverdale-isms. But ultimately, Clarkin seems to be playing along with, rather than trying to break free from the stereotypes of the genre and, to that extent, the song works effectively. Like 'The Tall Ships', it was performed live regularly in the 1994-95 period.

'Love's A Stranger' (5:11)
This is an intricate melodic rock song that showcases the band's considerable musical talent. It's dominated by a laid-back keyboard refrain that forms the basis for an accessible yet rather elaborately structured verse that segues neatly into the 'Love's a Stranger in this cruel world' pre-chorus/first chorus. The song moves up a notch with the brilliantly conceived guitar-drenched chorus, with more than a hint of Toto. Stanway's the star of this one, underlined by a dazzling (pan flute-sampling?) solo. It's another *Rock Art* tune that was a staple of the 1994-95 set and has also featured regularly at Kingdom of Madness gigs.

'Hush-A-Bye Baby' (4:48)
This is a long way from 'On A Storyteller's Night'. A soulful, old-school rock 'n' roll track, 'Hush-A-Bye Baby' is an indication of Clarkin's growing disquiet with what he considered, at the time, to be the narrow parameters of the Magnum sound. Jacki Graham and Mo Birch's backing vocals lend the song a distinct contemporary pop edge. A precursor of the style Clarkin would develop more fully with Hard Rain, it's interesting that, according to a December 1988 interview in *Raw* magazine, a version of the song was being considered for inclusion on the album that would become *Goodnight LA*.

'Just This Side Of Heaven' (4:20)
There are a few too many of these upbeat, lively – but ultimately one-paced – nuts-and-bolts rockers on the album. Despite a promising opening and an intense final minute of guitar acrobatics, the core of the song is disappointingly predictable.

'I Will Decide Myself' (4:15)
A nice change in pace for one of the few acoustic-based Magnum tracks (aside from *Keeping The Nite Light Burning*) since the early 1980s. This is a simple and soothing song, augmented by more effective pedal-steel work. It's pleasant enough but doesn't really go anywhere and there isn't quite the melodic quality of the band's other slower-paced tracks.

'On Christmas Day' (7:10)
To close the album, we have the final epic of the band's first phase, or of their career, as it seemed at the time. 'On Christmas Day' is a great track, a twisty First World War-themed multi-part companion piece to 1988's 'Don't Wake The Lion'. It focuses on the famous 1914 Christmas truce on the Western Front, where French, German and British soldiers crossed trenches and exchanged food, souvenirs and seasonal greetings in some sectors. More generally, the song explores one of Clarkin's core lyrical preoccupations: the futility of war.

Musically, this has all the hallmarks of the band's epic tracks, with changes of mood and time signature and an anthemic chorus. A shortened version of the song, presumably before 'The winds blow cold and hostile' section had been added, was played at the 1992 Christmas concert. In 2014, the song was re-recorded and released as a 10" single, with full-length and edited versions, to coincide with the centenary of the First World War. It remains a popular song with the fanbase, many of whom have established a tradition of playing it on 25 December every year.

Related Tracks
'You Don't Have To Be A Baby To Cry' (5:24)
A bonus track on 'The Tall Ships' CD single, this harks back to the 1980s Magnum sound, with the melody set even further in the past given its resemblance to a souped-up 'Stayin' Alive' (from *Magnum II*). It's less polished than some of the earlier material it recalls but is a powerful performance nonetheless. It should certainly have been included on *Rock Art* in place of one of the more generic hard rock numbers.

'Don't Start Me Talking' (2.40) (Sonny Boy Williamson II)
These two cover versions of 1950s rock 'n' roll hits, included as bonuses on the 'Back In Your Arms Again' CD single, are a fair indication of Clarkin's shifted focus by the end of the recording of *Rock Art*. The first, a full-blooded rendition of Sonny Boy Williamson's 1955 blues single (covered previously by

New York Dolls and Rory Gallagher, among others), is particularly impressive. Catley is on great form here, his voice soaring across this disturbing tale of marital strife and domestic abuse.

'Big Hunk Of Love' (2.58) (Aaron Schroeder and Sidney Wyche)
This is a pretty heavy and thoroughly enjoyable run-through of the Elvis Presley classic from 1959 (more accurately titled, 'A Big Hunk O' Love'). Although Catley thankfully avoids an Elvis impersonation, this version isn't a million miles away from the original, right down to Stanway's honky-tonk piano break. It sounds great but hardly warrants repeated listening.

The Split

Although there are variations in the precise story of why Magnum split up in 1995, the key factor was Tony Clarkin's desire to move on to new musical pastures. As he told Dave Ling at the time, 'Magnum takes up 24 hours of my life every day' which didn't allow him the time to try other things. He also felt restricted by having to write songs in a particular style and having, for instance, to include a lengthy prog-tinged epic on each album. Other factors, such as poor treatment by managers and record companies, had also clearly left Clarkin and other members of the band deeply disillusioned.

Stories that Clarkin's decision to leave had been prompted by a bust-up with keyboard player Mark Stanway, at the Rock and Blues Custom Show Festival in July 1995 surfaced some years later. Catley told *Rock Candy* magazine in 2021 that a 'big argument between Tony and another band member' prompted the guitarist to decide he'd had enough, while Clarkin himself has acknowledged that 'a lot of arguments were going on'.

Although there were rumours that the rest of the band might replace Clarkin with another guitarist, these were refuted by all concerned. To all intents and purposes, Magnum was over, save for *The Last Dance* farewell tour of Europe in October-December 1995, from which a live double album was released as *The Last Dance* by SPV in May 1996, and re-issued in 1997 in the UK by Receiver as *Stronghold* (see 'Live Albums').

Clarkin, meanwhile, had already written up to 11 tracks for what was meant to have been the next Magnum album. Instead, he took this collection of songs, along with sidekick Bob Catley, and repurposed them as the basis for what would become Hard Rain.

Breath Of Life (2002)

Personnel:
Tony Clarkin: guitars
Bob Catley: vocals
Mark Stanway: keyboards
Al Barrow: bass guitar
Produced at Mat Hat Studios, Coven, UK by Tony Clarkin
Engineer: Mark V. Stuart
Release date: 25 February 2002 on SPV/Steamhammer
Cover Design: Al Barrow
Highest chart places: UK, Germany and Sweden: Did not chart
Running time: 58:49

The idea for a Magnum reunion seems to have emerged in early 2000. Catley had left Hard Rain after the recording of their second album, *When The Good Times Come*, the previous year, to focus on his solo career. Clarkin aimed to carry on with Sue McCloskey as the main vocalist, but not much progress seems to have been made.

There have been some suggestions that the reunion was prompted by an upcoming 25-year anniversary – based on the time of the first recordings in 1976 rather than the date of 1972, which was officially recognised as the starting point of Magnum in later years. According to Clarkin, speaking to *eonmusic* in 2017, the idea hadn't occurred to him until he was contacted by his agent, Derek Kemp:

[He] had called me up and said: 'Why don't you put Magnum back together?' And I went: 'Who remembers Magnum?', I said: 'You tell me!' And he said he kept having calls and that people wanted to book the band. So I called Bob up and I said: 'What do you think, Bob, would you be interested in putting it back together?' and he went: 'YES, YES, YES!'

Catley: Yeah, I never thought we'd do this again, I thought it was over, so it was a complete shock.

Original members Clarkin and Catley remained at the core of the band, but there were attempts to reunite the 1990s line-up. Stanway, who had played sessions and set up his own drinks business during Magnum's hiatus, was asked to re-join early on in the process and happily returned to the fold. Drummer Mickey Barker was a different proposition. He was committed to folk rock band The Bushburys and was also playing regularly with notable 'Brum Beat' figures such as Trevor Burton and Steve Gibbons. Above all, he wasn't keen to go back out on the road. Clarkin contacted Barker and hoped he might change his mind but ultimately ran out of time and opted to record the album with computer-programmed drums.

Bass player Wally Lowe, meanwhile, had quit the music industry and emigrated to Spain and so was never an option. In his place, Magnum recruited Al Barrow, the bassist in Hard Rain who had also been playing with Catley's live solo band. In a 2022 interview with *Roppongi Rocks*, Barrow recalled the casual way in which he joined the band: 'There was not really a discussion of whether I was part of it or not; it just seemed to all fall in place. Tony said, "We'll start recording soon, so this is the plan: Now we are Magnum again". It was just a natural progression from Hard Rain to Magnum for me'.

The main label interested in signing the band was the German-based independent SPV, which had released *The Last Dance* live album in continental Europe back in 1996.

Recorded at Mad Hat Studios, now relocated from Walsall to Coven, near Wolverhampton, during the summer of 2001, *Breath Of Life* was an attempt to merge the 1990s Magnum sound with newer influences. In a press release, Clarkin stated that '[t]he tracks... basically have the same Magnum feel to them as earlier eras. But you can feel the amazing potential of modern studio technology as soon as you listen to the 12 tracks'. His main preoccupation, he informed John Callaghan of *Guitar* magazine, was to ensure that *Breath Of Life* didn't sound like a 1980s album, a revealing comment on his desire to move forward sonically, as well as his attitude towards the band's commercial peak a decade and a half earlier.

The closest similarities in sound are, not surprisingly, the *Sleepwalking* and *Rock Art* albums. But comparisons with Hard Rain are also obvious. Clarkin claimed that the new Magnum songs were 'more powerful, deeper and a little more passionate' than Hard Rain, which was certainly true. Yet many of the tracks on *Breath Of Life* are characteristic of the more upbeat vibe of Hard Rain, and the album as a whole is lighter and less rocky than most of the Magnum catalogue. The inclusion of two songs co-written with Sue McCloskey supports the idea propagated in later years by Catley that *Breath Of Life* was as much a Hard Rain as a Magnum album.

Reflecting back some years later, Clarkin noted how hard it had been to write for Magnum again: 'I thought to myself: "I can write a Magnum album – it's easy, it's like falling off a log... I thought I could do it really easily and I couldn't. I really had to concentrate on what I was doing'. As a result, *Breath Of Life* isn't an album that Clarkin is fond of. '[I]t's not a particularly good album', he noted in 2017, 'There's probably a couple of songs on it that are okay and the rest of it, I look back on it like: 'Oh my god!"

Clarkin's criticism of *Breath Of Life* is perhaps a little harsh. It's a flawed album, certainly, particularly in terms of its production, with the processed drums diminishing the power of many of the tracks and the guitars peripheral in the mix. But there's also a surprising amount of experimentation, along with the plethora of likeable tunes and hooks that Clarkin always managed to produce. The overall standard of songwriting is solid, even if the album contains few, if any, top-tier Magnum tracks.

The cover art is similarly flawed. It's a bit of a hotchpotch of ideas, not very well realised. Commenting to *Outsider Rock* in 2017, Barrow recalled the construction of the cover with mixed emotions:

> It was very rough and I said we can make this better in many ways but Tony said he liked how it looked and that is what he wanted to use. I asked are you sure? We can do better than this, but he liked the mosaic feel to it all. So he is the boss. But I look at it with a touch of fondness and regret.

Breath Of Life was originally intended as a double album, with an additional disc of older Magnum material. Eventually, it came out in most territories with three bonus tracks: live versions of 'The Flood (Red Cloud's War)' and 'Backstreet Kid', along with an acoustic rendering of 'We All Need To Be Loved'. A two-CD Japanese edition added live versions of 'It Must Have Been Love', 'Born To Be King' and 'Only A Memory'.

'Cry' (5:14)

A strange choice for the opening track of a reunion album, 'Cry', comes out of the traps at breakneck pace, eager to please but never quite convincing. An extended synth and orchestral introduction leads into a stuttering riff underpinned by an off-key guitar phrase. The verse is fairly standard melodic rock fare, but it's the chorus that really jars. The layered backing vocals, in particular, simply don't mesh with Catley's 'Take me down and down and down/Is there any place I can go?' refrain. Repeated listens have never smoothed things out to these ears. The middle eight attempts to up the drama but offers little melodic respite.

It may well be that 'Cry' was a conscious attempt to modernise the Magnum sound by incorporating some discordance and grunge styling. If so, it didn't really work, partly because the song remains essentially a classic rock tune with 1990s alternative rock trappings rather than an experimental amalgam of the two. 'Cry' featured prominently on the *Breath Of Life* tour but was subsequently dropped from the live set, never to return.

'This Heart' (4:03)

Things improve with this low-key track, more reminiscent of the 1990s albums but devoid of some of their power and polish. Beginning with more random sound collaging and agitated guitar swirls, 'This Heart' (originally 'This Heart Of Mine') soon settles into a more conventional Magnum style. As with much of the album, the keyboards take centre stage, adorned by Clarkin's riffs rather than vice-versa. The verse, in particular, proved that Clarkin had not lost his ability to write an effective hook, although the chorus is less memorable. As on much of the album, however, the production feels slight and strangely incomplete. The dynamics between sections are missing and the overall sound is flat and a tad bland. Had it been more sensitively produced, 'This Heart' could have been an album highlight, but here, it drifts away without making much of an impression.

'Everyday' (6.35)

In the years since its release, Bob Catley has suggested that *Breath Of Life* was a transitional album, halfway between the more commercial pop-rock of Hard Rain and the punchier and rockier pre-break-up Magnum sound. If that's so, 'Everyday' sits more in classic Magnum territory and is all the better for it. Mid-paced and (again) keyboard-heavy, it is the first (and possibly the only) song on the reunion album to come close to 'anthem' status. It benefits from a greater sensitivity to dynamics than is displayed elsewhere on the album, allowing for the big build-up and stirring chorus that was such a feature of Magnum's music during the 1980s and 1990s. It's a particular showcase for Catley, whose trademark clearly enunciated vocals propel the song along.

Nonetheless, it's not without its faults. Like a sizeable chunk of the band's 21st-century output, it's just a bit too long – a natural four-minute track extended to six-and-a-half minutes via a meandering opening and an interesting (but non-essential) mid-song instrumental breakdown. The band clearly regarded it as one of the album's highlights, featuring it prominently in the *Breath Of Life* tour and in festival appearances in 2002.

'Still' (Clarkin, Sue McCloskey) (4:03)

One of two tracks on the album to be co-written by Clarkin with former Hard Rain bandmate Sue McCloskey, 'Still' is another perfectly serviceable Magnum song hampered by poor production. In this case, the main culprit is the rather tinny, vanilla keyboard sound that dominates proceedings. It's a pleasant, upbeat track that might easily have fitted on a Hard Rain album, which is presumably where it was originally destined (a demo exists with McCloskey rather than Catley on lead vocals). The dreamy middle section suggests that Clarkin may have been borrowing some production techniques from his Shard End contemporary and fellow 'Brum Beat' alumni, Jeff Lynne.

'Dream About You' (Clarkin, Sue McCloskey) (4:16)

The second Clarkin/McCloskey co-write is a pretty competent ballad reminiscent of the slickest (and sickliest) of Aerosmith's 1990s efforts. It's a simple structure and the sentiments are in fairly standard love song territory; in this sense, it continues where the much superior 'Back In Your Arms Again' (from *Rock Art*) left off. There are some really nice touches. Catley's lived-in growl on the line, "Cause I can't have you liked I wanted to', is fabulously evocative and the chord change in the chorus (from B to C# minor) is lovely. Overall, however, there's not enough to lift this above any good-quality AOR ballad. One way of looking at 'Dream About You' (and the album's other ballad, 'Let Somebody In') is as Clarkin's writing practice for the more substantial lighter-in-the-air moments that were to feature on subsequent albums.

A remastered version (otherwise unchanged) was included as the opening track on the 2017 compilation, *The Valley Of Tears: The Ballads*.

'Breath Of Life' (4:48)
The title track is one of the more interesting tunes on the album. Aside from the opening keyboard chords, which echo the start of 'On A Storyteller's Night', this sounds quite unlike anything Clarkin has written for Magnum before. With its laid-back feel and bluesy guitar flourishes, it might be a lost Chris Rea or Mark Knopfler track. It's also the song that best incorporates the modern studio technology that Clarkin was so enamoured by. There's a lightness of touch in the production that's largely absent elsewhere on the record. The accentuated backing vocals at the end of the chorus, for instance, are unusual for Magnum but blend perfectly with the rest of the song.

The choice of 'Breath Of Life' as the title track may have been due to the 'We're back' sentiments of the lyrics: 'Here we are again/Always dream of places/Near and far/All those different faces'. But sonically, it's also a statement of intent, suggestive perhaps of how the 21st-century Magnum sound might develop.

'After The Rain' (4:03)
The fifth melodic, AOR-ish track in a row indicates that Clarkin was more comfortable in reviving that aspect of the band's sound than the hard rock elements. Nonetheless, it's another fine tune, with the highlight this time being Stanway's brilliant piano performance. The extended solo, in particular, is pure bombast, rekindling the crucial role that the keyboards played during the Jet years. Once again, the synthetic drums limit the power of what might otherwise have been a standout track. This is one of a number of songs on *Breath Of Life* that would also have benefitted from the re-recording afforded to 'That Holy Touch' and 'Just Like January' on the 2011 *Evolution* compilation.

'That Holy Touch' (5:12)
It's the hard rock tracks that suffer most from the album's lightweight production and 'That Holy Touch' is a case in point. The guitar riff, straight out of the Deep Purple songbook and not dissimilar to *Vigilante*'s 'Red On The Highway', is strong and the chorus is typically rousing. But the rhythm section, in particular, lacks punch and the song never really takes off as a result. Compare this to the version included on 2011's *Evolution*, with re-recorded drums, bass, guitars and some vocals. That one swings where the original plods. Structurally, the song isn't much different aside from some additional guitar flourishes and a new keyboard outro. But the re-recording sounds like a half-decent Magnum rocker, whereas the *Breath Of Life* version resembles a polished demo.

'Let Somebody In' (4:20)

'Let Somebody In' is, marginally, the better of the album's two ballads. Laid-back acoustic guitar and some nice vocal backing support another piano-heavy tune that plods along at a satisfactory pace. Clarkin produces one of his trademark short guitar solos, this one staying largely faithful to the vocal melody. The main problem with the song, however, is that it's all too predictable – some of the production touches that pepper other songs on the album might have lifted this one.

'The Face Of An Enemy' (3:48)

Rarely mentioned in reviews at the time, 'The Face Of An Enemy' is one of the album's more accomplished hard rock songs. Dominated by an exotic-sounding riff and some nicely used wah-wah effects, it's lifted by a punchy chorus melody. The chanted backing vocals are pretty lacklustre and the middle eight is short on drama, but overall, this is one of *Breath Of Life*'s more successful experiments. And at less than four minutes, it doesn't outstay its welcome.

'Just Like January' (4:30)

Another of the *Breath Of Life* tracks given a sonic facelift on 2011's *Evolution*, 'Just Like January' was good enough in its original version to be selected for live dates. A fairly conventional acoustic guitar and piano-dominated verse gives way to one of the album's more memorable choruses: 'Wolf cries by the river/Dark skies passing over/Soon deliver'. The *Evolution* version adds more aggressive guitar parts, punchy drums from Harry James and there are also improvements in the arrangement, with a shorter intro and a longer outro (including more convincing rain and thunder and telephone sound effects). Altogether, it sounds cleaner, crisper and more powerful than the *Breath Of Life* version.

'Night After Night' (7:56)

A slow-moving song with laid-back production, 'Night After Night' is not exactly the classic epic Magnum finale that was claimed at the time. There's nothing particularly complex here. It's a fairly standard Magnum composition, within which Clarkin gives himself rare space for some extended guitar noodling. Reviewing the album in *Classic Rock* magazine, Jerry Ewing considered 'Night After Night' to have 'that uplifting sense of hope prevalent in songs like 'The Spirit' and 'Les Morts Dansant''. Certainly, its relative simplicity and lyrical optimism serve as an upbeat conclusion to what is a fairly uneven reunion album.

Brand New Morning (2004)

Personnel:
Tony Clarkin: guitars
Bob Catley: vocals
Mark Stanway: keyboards
Al Barrow: bass
Harry James: drums
Produced at: Mad Hat Studios, Coven, UK by Tony Clarkin
Release date: 30 August 2004 on SPV/Steamhammer
Cover Design: Al Barrow/Generic Designs
Highest chart placings: UK, Germany and Sweden: Did not chart
Running time: 55:21

Brand New Morning was an important album for Magnum. The band's
reappearance had been welcomed by a core of dedicated fans, but *Breath
Of Life* represented a stuttering studio return. There were, nonetheless,
signs of an upturn in fortunes. The band recruited drummer Gary 'Harry'
James, formerly with hard rock act Thunder, who had split up in 1999, for
the 2002 live dates. James soon became a permanent band member (despite
the fact that he was also playing with a reformed Thunder from July 2002),
hardening the sound both live and in the studio. In addition, October 2003's
'Magnumania' convention held in Stourbridge, England, underlined the
strength and dedication of the band's fanbase.

In contrast to its ballad-heavy predecessor, *Brand New Morning* was a
harder-rocking, more guitar-oriented collection. As Catley told the *RockUnited*
website, the intention had been to create 'a big, epic rock album'. It's also
considerably darker, lyrically and visually, than *Breath Of Life*, and, indeed,
most of the band's previous output. Talking to *MelodicRock*, Catley agreed
that the album's themes and lyrics were dark but noted that this had, to some
extent, always been the case: 'We are a heavy lyric band. We are a rock band
that does lyrically heavy songs'.

According to Clarkin, the album had been relatively easy to record, with
James and Barrow completing the drum and bass parts for the whole album,
for example, in two days. That may be why it sounds a little rawer and more
sonically straightforward than Clarkin's previous production work.

The cover design, Barrow's second for the band, was a significant
improvement on the slightly amateurish *Breath Of Life*. Connected
thematically to both the title track and the album's concluding epic 'The
Scarecrow', the cover photograph is of a scrapyard at dawn (taken by Barrow
at Walsall, near Birmingham), with three wooden crosses superimposed on
the image. Two of the crosses have silhouetted scarecrows attached, while
the third cross is empty except for two crows; the returning scarecrow is in
the foreground of the image to the right, directly beneath the light emerging
from the moon. It was Catley who was dressed up and photographed as the

scarecrow, but his face wasn't shown clearly in any of the accompanying images. Once again, steering clear of previous logos, possibly with the aim of modernising the band's image, the visual presentation of both the band name and album title is a little uninspired.

More than a step in the right direction, *Brand New Morning* is one of the most powerful and cohesive albums of Magnum's career. It demonstrated that Clarkin had not lost his ability to craft intelligent and melodic hard rock and deserves to be considered in the same company as albums such as *Chase The Dragon* and *The Eleventh Hour* that helped define the band's sound.

'Brand New Morning' (6:17)
Catley and Clarkin have argued that *Brand New Morning* marked the 'real' return of Magnum, and it is the title track that most clearly supports that claim. It is a storming anthem in a similar vein to the band's harder-edged early classics like 'Kingdom Of Madness', 'Soldier Of The Line' and 'Vigilante'.

The album starts with an urgency that barely lets up. An atmospheric synth opening leads into a twisty guitar refrain, supported by pulsating bass and drums, closely echoing the famous beginning of AC/DC's 'Hell's Bells'. A minute and a half in, the song takes a left turn into a sludgy guitar riff that underpins the rest of the composition. This is a powerful piece of hard rock that highlights the importance of an effective rhythm section; it has an infectious groove that's even danceable at a push. And it's topped off by one of Clarkin's most inspired melodies.

Possibly influenced by the heart attack Clarkin had suffered at the Sweden Rock Festival in June 2002, the song's lyrics voice a desire to make the most of each day. 'It's like the first day of the rest of your life', Catley told *MelodicRock*, 'Forget everything else. Just wake up with the sun shining and start living. I only got one life'.

'It's Time To Come Together' (4:37)
Stanway's virtuoso keyboard playing is at the heart of this upbeat call for people to unite in spite of religious differences. The lively piano part dominates the track, blending neatly with understated wah-wah guitar, while Stanway and Clarkin also share soloing duties. In explaining the sentiments of the song, Catley referred to conflicts in Afghanistan and Iraq, admonishing people for 'arguing and fighting' on the basis of 'whose God is right' according to 'whatever religion you may be'. Simplistic and naïve as this approach may be, it chimes perfectly with the joyous energy of the track.

'We All Run' (4:53)
'We All Run' is one of the most immediate tracks on the album. Propelled by a majestic, keyboard-enhanced riff, it incorporates one of the band's very best sing-along hooks and highly effective apocalyptic imagery. At the time, Catley seemed to interpret the lyrical references to cities burning and angels at the

gates of heaven as a direct allusion to a nuclear holocaust. He also juxtaposed the almost speed or thrash metal lyrics with what he considered to be a light, 'party sing along' melody. As Clarkin explained to *MelodicRock*, however, the lyrics in the verse were really 'poetic licence' and the song was actually informed by the idea of people 'ignoring the important things in life'. The 'We All Run' sentiment was not meant to be literal but an indication that people simply didn't care enough about, and chose to ignore, the social and political problems of the day.

A live favourite, 'We All Run' was the only song apart from the title track to remain in the set for the *On A Storyteller's Night* 20th anniversary tour in 2005.

'The Blue And The Grey' (5:54)

This country-tinged track is one of *Brand New Morning*'s hidden gems. A laidback opening, which brings to mind superior New Age music, gives way to a sweeping cinematic tune good enough to stand alongside the very best of the band's 20th-century catalogue. There's nothing particularly complex or adventurous here, but Clarkin's beautiful, melancholic slide guitar work, augmented by a wonderfully expressive Catley vocal performance, is enough to set it apart as a highlight of a very strong album.

A variation on the futility of war theme, the song apparently focuses on the American Civil War, although there's nothing obvious to indicate this apart from the title. The reference to 'castle walls' may be nothing more than an allusion to the 'Solider Of The Line' lyrics. 'The Blue And The Grey' was played on the *Brand New Morning* tour but has not been heard live since.

'I'd Breathe For You' (6:27)

So consistent is Clarkin's writing on *Brand New Morning* that there are few dips in quality. If there is a weak spot on the record, however, it's probably this mid-paced stomper. It moves along pleasantly enough, driven by a solid riff which is echoed in the vocal melody. The imaginative interplay between keyboard and guitar – a feature of the album as a whole – is especially prominent in the chorus. The repeated assertions of the title in different vocal registers in the song's finale is another nice touch. For all this, 'I'd Breathe For You' is a track that feels slower than it is, lumbering where it might have marched. This isn't the fault of the rhythm section – which is bright and sparky throughout – so much as the fact that there just isn't enough going on in the track to sustain its six-and-half minutes. It's a trap Clarkin was, unfortunately, to fall into a number of times over the next few albums.

'The Last Goodbye' (6:28)

'The Last Goodbye' is, in some respects, another fairly standard, mid-paced rocker. But there are more ideas here, a greater diversity of sound, and, most importantly, a cracking melody to pull it through. There's a lovely piano introduction a la 'Sacred Hour' before the track comes to life via Quoesque chugging guitars. A nice bridge into one of Clarkin's typically hook-heavy choruses follows with more than a passing resemblance to 'Vigilante'. Described to *RockUnited* as 'an up-tempo sad song', the whole thing holds together well, helped in no small part by James' tight and steady drumming. One of the album's highlights, it was played throughout the *Brand New Morning* tour.

'Immigrant Son' (5:35)

The pace quickens for the next two numbers, both of which deserve greater recognition in the Magnum catalogue. Catley described 'Immigrant Son' at the time as the story of 'a chap coming out from somewhere in Europe, to England actually, and starting a new life, like a lot of people are now'. The song sensibly eschews any direct political statement, focusing instead on the experience of migration, travel and belonging from the migrants' point of view. The notion of the 'endless journey', involving an inevitable return to the station 'some day' and 'always waiting' paints a picture of hardship and struggle, although there are hints of optimism in the suggestion that the migrant can ultimately 'be what you wanted to be'.

Musically, this is one of the album's heavier moments, dominated by thrashy guitar riffing and James' energetic drumming. The chorus, with one of Clarkin's trademark circular structures, is tightly harmonised and beautifully delivered by Catley. The *Evolution* version with re-recorded guitars and drums is slightly brighter sonically but feels less powerful than the original.

'Hard Road' (5:21)

This is another deep-cut hard rock jewel in the Magnum catalogue. The sharp contrast between the light pop-rock of the verse and the hard-hitting chorus is highly effective, nodding subtly to different phases in the band's past. While the gorgeous melody of the verse recalls the hits of the *Vigilante* and *Wings Of Heaven* period, the crunching power of the chorus's descending chord structure brings to mind the heavier material of the Jet era. The two are combined to great effect here and are topped off by an imaginative coda featuring atmospheric backward guitar and vocal effects. 'Hard Road' is an album highlight that manages to pay due respect to the established Magnum sound while offering something fresh and inventive.

'The Scarecrow' (9:50)

The second longest song in the Magnum catalogue, 'The Scarecrow' is an interesting but ultimately flawed attempt to revisit the epic compositions of the band's first phase. A laidback piano and keyboard introduction provides the song with its texture, supported by a lovely, scurrying bass line. At around a minute and a quarter, crashing guitar chords are introduced. The 'Where we go he can't follow/He's got to stay' chorus refrain is another strong melody line, buttressed by thick backing vocals to give maximum effect here. The song stretches out for another five minutes, interspersed only by a short, jazzy interlude and a guitar break. At around 8.22, there's a last-minute change of pace, with chugging guitar and a different vocal line. It's a pleasant but unremarkable coda and does feel a little as if it's been bolted on. While 'The Scarecrow' is a solid, listenable track in which Magnum channel their love of (contemporary) 1970s hard rock acts like Uriah Heep, it doesn't quite have the depth and quality to rank alongside multi-part epics such as 'Don't Wake The Lion', 'On Christmas Day' and 'In The Beginning'.

Lyrically, the song can be taken in a number of ways: as a literal tale of a scarecrow that gets down from his perch and walks; a metaphor for hope in the face of sadness and adversity; or a more overtly religious parable. The obvious Christian imagery of the lyrics – as well as the album cover – were acknowledged by Catley at the time, who admitted that the song included 'a little religious content'. More specifically, there are similarities with a passage from the Old Testament's Book of Jeremiah, comparing false idols (such as Christmas trees) to scarecrows in a cucumber field, that can't speak or move and yet shouldn't be feared. It may be, however, that the song simply uses the figure of the scarecrow to represent vaguely spiritual or Christian values, such as peace, hope and courage.

Related Tracks
'Dreamland' (5:37)
A lengthy ballad included as a bonus on the Japanese edition, this was apparently left off the album because it didn't fit with the guitar-oriented material that constituted the bulk of the collection. It's an unusual Clarkin composition, not so much in its relaxed mood and romantic imagery, as in its relative restraint and simplicity. It's a song that drifts along with little of the bombast of some of the band's better-known ballads. For its uniqueness in the Magnum catalogue if nothing else, it's a bit of a shame that 'Dreamland' was tucked away as a Japanese bonus track.

Princess Alice And The Broken Arrow (2007)

Personnel:
Tony Clarkin: guitars
Bob Catley: vocals
Mark Stanway: keyboards
Al Barrow: bass
Jimmy Copley: drums
Additional musicians:
Jim Lea: violin on 'You'll Never Sleep'
Produced at: M2, Mad Hat Studios, Coven, UK, by Tony Clarkin
Release date: 26 March 2007 on SPV/Steamhammer
Cover design: Rodney Matthews
Highest chart places: UK: 70, Germany: 60, Sweden: Did not chart
Running time: 62:47

Although it was their third album since reforming, *Princess Alice And The Broken Arrow* is sometimes regarded as the start of a new era for Magnum. If *Brand New Morning* had demonstrated that Clarkin could still produce inventive material that straddled the line between hard rock and melodic rock, the *On A Storyteller's Night* anniversary tour in 2005, in which the 1985 album was played in its entirety, reminded the band what they were aiming for.

The 2005 tour, immortalised in the *Living The Dream* DVD, was considered a great success and also introduced a new drummer in Jimmy Copley. He stepped in for Harry James when it became clear that Thunder's touring commitments were going to clash with Magnum's. Copley was a highly respected session musician who had worked with Jeff Beck, Killing Joke, Tears For Fears, Go West, Paul Rodgers and Tony Iommi, among many others. He was also a well-known exponent of open-handed drumming, a technique that eschews the conventional crossing of the hands when playing the hi-hat and snare drum simultaneously.

Despite this injection of fresh talent, *Princess Alice* was an album that looked backwards as well as forwards. The influence of *On A Storyteller's Night* can be detected across the album. It is perhaps most evident in the fantasy title and the return of Rodney Matthews' artwork. The title itself combines two different ideas. Princess Alice refers to an orphanage near Sutton Coldfield, just outside Birmingham, where one of Clarkin's distant relatives had been brought up. Opened in 1883 by the National Children's Home, the Princess Alice Orphanage operated for almost 100 years until its closure in 1982. 'You'll Never Sleep', the final track on the album, alludes to the orphanage, as we will see below, and was originally titled 'Princess Alice'. The 'Broken Arrow' part of the title is linked to the song 'Like Brothers We Stand', about the treatment of Native Americans, particularly the breaking of the arrow as a customary sign of peace.

The two ideas are linked in what appears to be a completely unconnected fantasy cover scene. The *Alice In Wonderland*-like Princess Alice character, who is breaking an arrow above her head, sits at the left side of the table with a malevolent, well-dressed fox chuckling away at the other end; in the background are children in cages, recalling *The Eleventh Hour* cover. More specifically, the wood-panelled room in which the scene is set and the table positioned at the centre of the image, nod to Matthews' *Storyteller's Night* cover.

Storyteller's Night clearly also influenced the musical palette of *Princess Alice*. Catley told *Fireworks* magazine that the songs on the new album were a conscious effort by Clarkin to revisit the band's past in view of the interest that the 20th-anniversary tour had generated. 'The songs aren't the same', he noted, 'but there are songs on this album that are reminiscent of some... on the *On A Storyteller's Night* album'. Although there is no attempt to provide a carbon copy of the 1985 album, there's also no doubt that that collection provides some of the inspiration for the melodic epics on *Princess Alice*, such as 'When We Were Younger', 'Dragons Are Real' and 'You'll Never Sleep'.

The 'Making Of' DVD, which came with the limited first edition of the CD, provides a rare commentary on a Magnum album from all members of the band (with the exception of Copley). Stanway thought that the record had an organic, earthy sound and, interestingly, noted that Clarkin was open to the rest of the band interpreting the instrumental lines he'd written, something that the keyboardist later complained was not true of other albums. In Barrow's view, his use of a 5-string bass guitar added warmth and depth to the bottom end of the recording. Barrow also noted the influence of Peter Gabriel's music and Gabriel bassist Tony Levin's playing in his own contributions to the record. Interestingly, both Stanway and Barrow observed, in relation to different songs, that Clarkin had asked them to simplify their parts, which they agreed had benefitted the recording. Clarkin's main observation of *Princess Alice* as a whole was that he 'felt free' to write what he wanted on the album.

Princess Alice ended up as a turning point for the band. It was the first post-reformation album to break the Top 100 in the UK, reaching number 70, and was more successful still in the band's other core market, Germany, where it made number 60. The quality of the melodies match *Brand New Morning*, and the recording is a little less muddy, but the side-lining of the band's rockier side, and the overloading of mid-paced tracks, means it also lacks the diversity of its predecessor. Nonetheless, the whole package – complete with a new logo, Matthews' fifth for the band – showed that Magnum were willing to embrace their past, or at least certain elements of it, and acknowledge their fantasy side alongside the realism of Clarkin's lyrics.

'When We Were Younger' (7:00)
This is the first in a series of Clarkin compositions, across this and subsequent albums, that reflect on aspects of the past. There's a heavy whiff of nostalgia

in the lyrics as the narrator remembers friends, acquaintances and lovers from childhood and adolescence, wondering 'where are they now?' and considering how time changes people, places and relationships. The chorus is an ode to the simpler life:

When we were younger we lived for the day
They seemed much longer but drifted away
Now I'm much older, I don't have to try
There's no one to whisper goodbye.

The lyrics specifically recall a trip Clarkin took to the area in which he grew up in Birmingham, literally walking the street 'where we all used to live' and where he was concerned to find that, 'there's nothing the same' as it used to be. In the wrong hands, this could be cliché-ridden and overly sentimental, but the genuine emotion in the lyrics and Catley's delivery ensures that this is a thoughtful and moving song.

As on much of the album, there's a restrained and laid-back feel, which is rare in the band's catalogue. Opening with a looped keyboard phrase and delicate piano, the song gathers momentum in the bridge and through the galloping rhythm of the chorus. It's characterised by some lovely acoustic guitar work by Clarkin, especially the lilting solo after the second chorus. Above all, it benefits from an especially strong melody and a simple, unfussy production. 'When We Were Younger' was one of the few songs on *Princess Alice* to have lasted beyond the album tour and remained a live favourite over a decade later, even featuring on 2018's *Live At Symphony Hall* album.

'Eyes Wide Open' (5:54)
Catley's favourite song on the album at the time of recording, 'Eyes Wide Open' combines heavy riffing with subtle acoustic guitar lines. It's an elegantly constructed track, underpinned by great drumming from Copley and topped off with another catchy melody delivered at what seems to be near the top of Catley's register. The lyrics are a tad elusive, although Martin Vielhaber has claimed that they concern the aftermath of war. 'Eyes Wide Open' is one of a number of tracks on the album that reminds the listener of the subtle blending of melody and atmosphere that marked out *Storyteller's Night*. As one of the most complete tracks on the album, it's something of a surprise that it didn't make the live set.

'Like Brothers We Stand' (5:35)
This is Clarkin's second attempt (after *Sleepwalking*'s 'The Flood') at exploring the treatment of indigenous Americans. Written from the perspective of the exploited victims, the lyrics are direct but effective, highlighting not just the deception and violence of the white aggressors but also their failure to appreciate the indigenous worldview: 'They didn't realise they were

the strangers/How could they think so small?' Musically, this is a pretty straightforward acoustic-based track. There aren't too many frills and it relies on the clarity of the delivery and the strength of the melody. But it is one of Clarkin's very best tunes, with an equally catchy verse and chorus. Magnum weren't releasing singles by this time, but a CD promo did appear in Germany, including a radio edit (stripped of some of the instrumental passages and the guitar solo) along with 'Your Lies'.

'Out Of The Shadows' (6:58)

An anti-war song with a twist, 'Out Of The Shadows' focuses on the futility of conflict but also the role of human scavengers in the aftermath of major battles. Sometimes associated with the 18th and 19th-century resurrectionists, who were grave robbers employed by anatomists to exhume recently buried corpses, scavengers followed troops around the battlefields of Europe. As well as looting the body for clothes and valuables, some brought pliers with them to remove the dead men's teeth, which, in the early days of cosmetic dentistry, could be a valuable commodity. The teeth of healthy young men were particularly prized in making 'natural' dentures. Large quantities were shipped back to Britain after 1815 and were popularly known as 'Waterloo Teeth'. Clarkin's grisly tale sketches the role of these 'resurrectionists' and 'scavengers' who emerge 'out of the shadows' to 'get rich' from the 'fifty-thousand [who] lay dead'. The final line of the song pointedly refers to 'the final demand' of 'Waterloo teeth from the ghost of a man'.

'Out Of The Shadows' is one of the album's few straight-ahead rock tracks. Clarkin's angular riff resembles the guitar lines of Scorpions' Matthias Jabs and is complemented by a particularly tight rhythm section, with Copley, especially, on fine form. It adds some beef to what is emerging as a fairly light album. At nearly seven minutes, however, it's longer than it needs to be.

'Dragons Are Real' (5:21)

This is another track sporting a memorable Clarkin melody that completes one of the best first sides (in vinyl terms) of a Magnum record for many years. There's an urgency in the bass playing and drumming, topped off by Stanway's keyboard groove. A typically impassioned Catley vocal narrates the tale of a youngster in his bedroom immersed in a fantasy book, reading about 'all the princes and kings/Soldiers at war doing treacherous things'. As well as an ode to the power of imagination (and another track that nostalgically celebrates aspects of childhood), it's a subtle dig at the lazy journalists and music critics who wrote Magnum off as a 'dungeons and dragons' band based on a handful of cover illustrations or one or two early tracks. The title also, consciously or subconsciously, reflects back on music paper adverts for the *Chase The Dragon* album in 1982, which had included the statement, 'Dragons Aren't Real'. Some writers, such as long-time supporter Dave Ling, didn't like the track at all, possibly missing the intricacy of the message and choosing not to be won over by the song's melodic simplicity. Yet, more than any other song on the album, 'Dragons Are Real' realised SPV's marketing description of the record as 'a luxurious sonic experience that invites its listeners to dream away to'.

'Inside Your Head' (6:01)
Clarkin describes this in the 'Making Of' DVD as an offshoot from the 'Princess Alice' idea and so a kind of companion piece to the final track, 'You'll Never Sleep'. It was inspired by a meeting the guitarist had with an elderly relative he hadn't seen for years and the imagined thoughts of past experiences and missed opportunities. It's a poignant, slightly sedate ballad with a fairly sparse arrangement. Stanway notes in the 'Making Of' DVD that he was encouraged to simplify the keyboard parts in the manner of John Lennon. But this is no 'Imagine' and the song suffers from not having enough going on to hold the listener's attention. The melody is simply not strong enough to carry the song alone.

'Be Strong' (5:40)
The album moves in a slightly harder direction with this high-energy rocker built on an insistent Copley drum shuffle. Clarkin throws in a catchy descending riff and choppy guitars to go along with the funky bass work and keyboard embellishments. The song touches on one of Clarkin's favourite lyrical motifs – the power of individuals to choose their own way in life and fight for what they want. It's a positive enough statement that, nonetheless, lacks the depth of some of the best material on the album.

'Thank You For The Day' (5:10)
This is one of the tracks on *Princess Alice* that clearly harks back to the band's 1980s sound. It's a swinging, melodic, pumped-up anthem that can be interpreted as a salute to important individuals as well as the fanbase: as Clarkin put it, 'if someone does something great for you, thanks for making the day wonderful'. Clarkin notes on the 'Making Of' DVD that the lyrics came to him when he was singing along to the instrumental tracks in the car. Given its sentiments, it's not surprising that it became a popular, if short-lived, live track. It was also popular within the band. Stanway situated it in a long line of Magnum anthems while Barrow saw it as an 'emotionally powerful epic'.

'Your Lies' (4:54)
Boasting a killer Deep Purple/Dio-esque riff, this is the best of the album's hard rock tunes. Clarkin's songwriting nous is clearly in evidence here, with one of his familiar key shifts from the introduction to the verse and a change of tempo to a neatly constructed slow middle eight. It's topped off with a short and sweet guitar solo that underlines Clarkin's long-standing preference for melody over technique. The song is a sardonic swipe at the behaviour

of politicians, which was to become a favourite Clarkin subject in the post-reunion period. The lines, 'We're all pigs at the same trough/Dealing while we're praying', even nod towards the social commentary of Pink Floyd's Roger Waters.

'Desperate Times' (5:22)
It may be one of the least celebrated songs on the album, but this is far from filler. An almost joyous composition that doesn't quite seem to fit with the title, 'Desperate Times' starts off as a middling mid-paced number but builds into classic Magnum bombast. The chorus sounds especially big, augmented by power chords, multi-layered backing vocals and Copley's drum rolls. 'Desperate Times' is another melodic jewel on one of the band's most melodious albums.

'You'll Never Sleep' (4:57)
Princess Alice concludes with not only the best track on the album but one of the best in the band's entire catalogue. It's a serious and emotionally wrought contemplation on memory, guilt and family, based on research Clarkin himself undertook on his family history and one particular relative who had spent time at the Princess Alice orphanage. The reference to lives buried away for 'a hundred years' alludes to the UK rule that personal information contained in census records cannot be made available to the public for that period of time. The musical bleakness of the verse is offset by the barnstorming bridge and chorus, to which former Slade bassist Jim Lea contributes some stirring violin lines. Amazingly, 'You'll Never Sleep' was another song that was left off the *Princess Alice* tour (though it was featured on the second leg of the *Wings Of Heaven* anniversary tour) and has, therefore, never been accorded the significance in the Magnum canon that it rightly deserves.

Into The Valley Of The Moonking (2009)

Personnel:
Tony Clarkin: guitars
Bob Catley: vocals and tambourine
Mark Stanway: keyboards
Al Barrow: bass and backing vocals
Harry James: drums
Additional musicians:
Jim Lea: violins, violas and cellos in 'Blood On Your Barbed Wire Thorns'
Sheena Sear: string arrangement for 'Blood On Your Barbed Wire Thorns'
Produced at: M2, Mat Hat Studios, Coven, UK by Tony Clarkin
Engineers: Mark Stuart and Sheena Sear
Release date: 12 June 2009 in Germany; 15 June 2009 in the rest of Europe on
SPV/Steamhammer
Cover Design: Rodney Matthews
Highest chart places: UK: 82, Germany: 59, Sweden: 41
Running time: 58:10

After the *Princess Alice* tour, Magnum embarked on another 20th-anniversary celebration of one of its landmark 1980s albums, *Wings Of Heaven*. The band played the 1988 record in its entirety, along with a selection of recent and older favourites, across dates in the UK in November and December 2007 and then again in the UK and continental Europe in May 2008 to support the just-released *Wings Of Heaven Live* recording.

On this occasion, however, the band's re-familiarisation with their 1980s material had a less obvious influence on the next studio recording. Instead, *Into The Valley Of The Moonking* revisits the melodic rock template laid down by *Princess Alice*. It is more guitar-heavy and a little rockier than its predecessor but is similarly dominated by mid-paced material. Yet, whereas *Princess Alice* boasts some genuine surprises and a plethora of excellent melodies, *Moonking* is a more one-dimensional and patchy collection of songs. Although it has its moments, it's ultimately a fairly lacklustre affair, on par with *Breath Of Life* as the weakest album of the reunion period.

The band, however, were very positive about *Moonking* at the time. Clarkin considered it 'more complete' than the band's earlier work: 'it seems that it's taken me 25 years to learn how to do it properly'. Meanwhile, an unusually high six songs – 'Cry To Yourself', 'All My Bridges', 'Take Me To The Edge', 'The Moonking', 'No One Knows His Name' and 'A Face In The Crowd' – were played onstage regularly on the accompanying UK and European tours.

Clarkin outlined the process of writing and selecting songs in an interview with Get Ready to Rock radio at the time of the album's release. Rather than revisit demos from previous writing sessions, he started from scratch, writing songs with no particular theme or agenda in mind for what the album should sound like. Over the course of more than a year (presumably in gaps between touring from mid-2007 until around the autumn of 2008), Clarkin amassed something in the region of 60 song ideas at home using drum samples and basic bass, keyboard and guitar parts. These were whittled down to around 15-20 tracks that were then taken into the studio with proper guitar parts added, at which time, Clarkin brought Catley in to listen and the two honed the material down to a more manageable 55-60 minutes.

The title emerged from a jotting Catley found in one of the guitarist's lyric books. Clarkin had been intent on providing the album with a fantasy title and theme similar to its predecessor, and had experimented with various combinations, such as '...and the Black Orchid'. Resurrected from his lyric book, the 'Moonking' idea was combined with the Valley of the Rocks in Exmoor, North Devon, close to where he used to live, to create *Into The Valley Of The Moonking*. Clarkin settled on the title because, as he told the *Shropshire Star* newspaper, 'To me, it sounded magical'. As was common by this time, the album title was chosen after the music but before most of the words had been written and was meant to inspire Clarkin to 'fly off and write all these lyrics'.

The cover was, again, a Rodney Matthews creation with plenty of input from Clarkin. The main image, according to the guitarist, was inspired by English author Enid Blyton's 'Famous Five' juvenile books, which told old-fashioned tales of childhood adventure. It depicts a schoolboy, replete with cap, stripy blazer and catapult in his back pocket, being shown the way to a mysterious world (presumably the valley of the album title) by a benevolent 'Moses-like' figure. Also portrayed in the image are a dragon and lion, purportedly representing heaven and earth, and the castle from *Chase The Dragon* in the far distance. The whole scene is contained in a circular frame with mysterious writing and markings around it. The painting is less intricate than many of Matthews' Magnum covers, but it is one of the most effective, even if the band name and album title are rendered in rather uninspired script lettering.

'Intro' (1:30)
Stanway's short cinematic keyboard introduction, complete with windswept sound effects, does an effective job of encapsulating the fantasy stylings of the cover and the album title. It's a promising opening that hints at an expansive and progressive sound that the rest of the album, unfortunately, fails to take up.

'Cry To Yourself' (4:40)
Emerging from Stanway's keyboard intro, 'Cry To Yourself' is a meat-and-potatoes guitar-led track with some nice touches but lacks the epic feel of many of the band's album openers. While the main melody line is likeable and Catley delivers the vocal with customary aplomb, the main problem here is the tempo of the performance. Clarkin has noted that the speed of Magnum songs can alter significantly in the writing and recording process. Here, the

pace of the track seems unnaturally slow, which is especially evident in the clanging guitar chords that dominate the chorus. Unusually for Magnum, there's an absence of energy in the playing (James' drum fills aside) and variety in the arrangement. Simple instrumental lines can be effective, but there's just not enough variety in this song to sustain the listener's interest.

'All My Bridges' (4:41)
If Clarkin did draw on *Wings Of Heaven* influences for the writing of *Moonking*, it seems they were all distilled into this one track. It begins with Stanway arpeggios à la Elton John's version of 'Pinball Wizard', which then morphs into a punchy 1980s pop metal riff. The chord change into the verse mirrors a similar transposition in 'Days Of No Trust'. Yet, there's an energy and invention to the track that ensures it's much more than the sum of its influences. Not only is it the best tune on the album, but it's delivered with confidence and ebullience. It's a rare recognition by Clarkin that the more overtly commercial side of the Magnum sound was, and still is, a key part of their DNA.

'Take Me To The Edge' (4:17)
This is the type of fast, punchy hard rock number that the band have often tried to pull off but rarely managed. It's elevated by some fine Clarkin lead guitar and Catley at his raspy best. Yet, in Magnum's hands, this sort of track seems to lack a bit of authenticity, as if the band are playing up to the hard rocking credentials of contemporaries such as Saxon and UFO rather than being themselves.

'The Moonking' (6:16)
One of the high points of the album, the (almost) title track, is a bluesy concoction that acts as a vehicle for Clarkin, in particular, to show off his technical chops. But it's also a really effective and unusual song, mixing blues licks with fantasy imagery. The verses are understated and sparsely arranged, allowing space for Clarkin to extemporise with feeling and sensitivity. As the song builds, it moves into more familiar anthemic territory towards a layered chorus, which includes one of the band's most simple yet affecting melodies. It's a wonderfully expressive track that brings out a fine Catley vocal performance, although it's doubtful whether even the singer knows what the references to 'Celtic twilight', 'warm solar winds' and 'bright silver skies' actually mean.

'No One Knows His Name' (4:32)
Although far from unlistenable, the middle run of tracks on *Moonking* constitutes one of the least remarkable sections of the band's catalogue. 'No One Knows His Name' is a brooding examination of the attitude towards the unknown dead in wartime, a theme that Clarkin was to return to again on

tracks such as 'Unwritten Sacrifice' from *Escape From The Shadow Garden*. There's a neat tempo change into the chorus, which also includes an enjoyable Stanway counter-melody. But the fact that the most interesting part of the track is the extended stage ending speaks volumes.

'In My Mind's Eye' (5:42)

This is another well-constructed track hampered by a ponderous tempo that sucks out most of its energy. Once again, the most interesting sections – such as the atmospheric middle eight and Catley's vocal embellishments in the final minute – are those that offer something above and beyond the steady march that constitutes most of the track. Some of the lyrics, such as the 'I don't want money, I don't want fame' line, are clearly autobiographical. As Clarkin told the *Shropshire Star*, 'a lot of people know that I'm like that anyway. I just thought I'd put that down just for the record'.

'Time To Cross That River' (5:17)

A semi-ballad featuring lilting piano and a lovely acoustic guitar solo, 'Time To Cross That River' is a pleasant song but without the oomph to lift the mid-album rut. The chess-themed lyric, possibly influenced by the 'Your Move' section of Yes' 'I've Seen All Good People', works reasonably well, with the final lines of the chorus – 'Heroes we've seen come and go through the years/ Nothing is just black and white' – being particularly inventive. The inclusion of orchestral concert sound effects, applause and mid-song audience chatter is also a nice production trick that would be revisited for later recordings.

'If I Ever Lose My Mind' (4:19)

There's a slight upturn in quality for this dark, atmospheric and weighty composition. It's another of the album's mid-paced tracks, but this one really cranks up the mood with the ominous, slowly unwinding chord progression in the verse. The chorus is fine, but the main appeal of the track is in the verse.

'A Face In The Crowd' (6:24)

This is a superior Clarkin ballad, probably his best since 'Back In Your Arms Again' from *Rock Art*. Lyrically, it dwells on one of his favourite themes: believing in one's self and persevering in spite of the challenges life throws up. Musically, it's an uncomplicated but expertly crafted composition with a huge chorus, including a simple yet deeply touching vocal line. Clarkin follows power ballad rules in shifting key for the guitar solo and, as with his best songs, it includes a middle eight, which is just as good as the verse and the chorus.

'Feels Like Treason' (3:32)

This is the heaviest song on the album; a spiky, sparky, but ultimately fairly conventional hard rock number. In an album full of fairly sedate, contemplative material, this is a welcome change of pace, but it might have worked better sequenced a little earlier to lift the mid-album trough.

'Blood On Your Barbed Wire Thorns' (6:57)

The final track is the album's most controversial among die-hard fans. The replica AC/DC riff and 'Yeah, Yeah, Yeah' chants in the chorus are not exactly common Magnum fare, simulating traditional hard rock tropes rather than the more cerebral approach generally associated with the band. But what it does offer is an element of variety and exhilaration that is missing from large chunks of a disappointingly one-paced album.

'Blood On Your Barbed Wire Thorns' is a song of two halves. The no-nonsense rock tune that takes up the first four and a half minutes sees the band experimenting with sounds and rhythms as they had done on 1994's *Rock Art*. Augmented by jaunty Stanway piano accompaniment, this is an effective and enjoyable section, whether seen on its own terms or as a pastiche. The second half is almost a different track entirely; a beautifully crafted instrumental featuring laid-back guitar melodies and dreamy keyboard passages, given added depth by Jim Lea's stirring strings. It's an inspired and surprising end to an otherwise fairly pedestrian album.

The Visitation (2011)

Personnel:
Tony Clarkin: guitars and backing vocals
Bob Catley: vocals
Mark Stanway: keyboards
Al Barrow: bass and backing vocals
Harry James: drums
Additional musicians:
Jim Lea: strings
Sheena Sear: String Arrangements
Produced at: M2 Studios, Coven, UK by Tony Clarkin
Engineers: Sheena Sear and Mark Stuart
Release date: 14 January 2011 on SPV/Steamhammer
Cover Illustration: Rodney Matthews/Al Barrow
Highest chart places: UK: 55, Germany: 19, Sweden: 28
Running time: 57:01

The Visitation continued the consistency of the reunion albums but struck out in new directions as well. Although it maintained the trend towards a heavier, more guitar-oriented sound, Clarkin's full-throttle riffs are utilised within songs that keep melody to the fore. *The Visitation* also incorporates more experimental and progressive sections than were evident in either of the previous two albums and includes full-blown string arrangements on two tracks.

Clarkin was obviously mindful of the danger of the band sounding predictable and one-dimensional and so tried to vary the sound and mood within and between songs. He pointed to two other changes that he thought had improved the quality of the album's production. First of all, bassist Al Barrow was brought in for backing vocals (though he was similarly credited on *Moonking*) to give 'a different texture' than on previous albums, where Catley had taken care of all backing as well as lead vocals. Secondly, at M2 Studios, Sheena Sear took over primary engineering duties, a change significant enough for Clarkin to specifically acknowledge in the liner notes as well as interviews at the time. Mark Stuart remained the band's live sound engineer (and later tour manager) but, from this point on, took a secondary role in the studio.

These changes were certainly vindicated because *The Visitation* is a more memorable album than the somewhat disappointing *Moonking*. The rhythm section of Al Barrow and Harry James was now beginning to sound more confident, while the core of Clarkin, Stanway and Catley were putting in stellar performances on par with the 1980s albums. Above all, Clarkin was developing into an increasingly consistent songwriter, characterised by the reflective lyrics and sophisticated arrangements that would come to define the band over the next decade.

It wasn't entirely well received, however. *Classic Rock*'s Malcolm Dome, one of the band's long-standing supporters, wrote a scathing review that dismissed the songs as forgettable and the performances as 'lacklustre': 'It's as if the band are going through the motions and aren't quite sure why they're in the studio'.

The Visitation was the third album in a row to feature a Rodney Matthews sleeve, although, this time, it was used alongside an Al Barrow illustration on the boxset and CD digipack. Based on the 'Doors To Nowhere' lyrics reflecting on the band's childhood, Matthews' surrealistic depiction of a room containing a range of symbolic objects is unusual for a Magnum sleeve. But it's one of his most visually striking illustrations. As was becoming common, there are allusions to previous album covers – such as the school cap and catapult of the boy on *Moonking* and the storyteller's staff and bag (with 'Who is the Storyteller?' scribbled on the wall). A sword of chaos rests on the wall on the left of the room and swords of chaos are printed above the windows on the right, with a picture of the *Wings Of Heaven Live* sleeve in between. A wooden heart is at the centre of the picture with a map of the United Kingdom and three nails driven in around the Birmingham area where the core band members grew up – possibly referencing the lyrics of both 'Doors To Nowhere' and 'The Last Frontier'. The illustration also shares similarities to one of Matthews' rejected drawings for 1986's *Vigilante* sleeve.

Matthews' website indicates that he had expected his illustration to be the front cover 'and was surprised to see it tucked away inside the album package'. Barrow's front cover depicts a timepiece design based on a broach Clarkin used to wear on his jacket. The band reverted to the *Vigilante* logo that had last been used on *Rock Art*. Initially, they had wanted the logo to be in black so that it could only be seen as the album was moved around, but it was eventually rendered in more conventional gold at the top of the cover.

'Black Skies' (5:53)
'Black Skies' is a slow-building monster of a tune that maintains a new trend for epic album openers dating back to *Brand New Morning*. Sonically, it is a close relation to the 2004 title track, with a similar rhythmic pattern and brooding menace. It is, however, much heavier. Clarkin was apparently concerned at the time of the album's release that it might prove too heavy for existing fans.

Soft cymbals join with pulsating keyboards until the guitar kicks in at around the 45-second mark. The chord changes and vocal melody are solid, if unspectacular and it's the guitar riff that really maintains the momentum. More electronic-style keyboard patterns from Stanway usher in a dreamy middle section that offers some respite but is soon extinguished by the vocal: 'Gone as the sunlight fades/My eyes with sorrow/And without warning kills/ The flame of tomorrow'. We shouldn't be surprised that a song titled 'Black Skies' offers little hope, but this is an unusual synergy of dark music and lyrics by Magnum standards.

Another anti-war song, 'Black Skies', also became a live staple on *The Visitation* tour and then again on 2014's *Escape From The Shadow Garden* tour, where it was often played second following that album's opening track, 'Live 'Til You Die'.

'Doors To Nowhere' (5:43)

There's an immediate change of pace with this sprightly number. Clarkin's sparky riff ('Eye Of The Tiger', anyone?) heralds an interesting composition that moves between a laid-back keyboard-driven verse and a quicker and rockier two-part chorus section. In less experienced hands, the shifts in tempo might seem awkward and contrived, but here, it's effortless. Overall, the song works really well, held down by James' pinpoint drumming and a solid Barrow bass line. It also features an extended Clarkin guitar solo and a bonus mini-solo at the end of the song.

Lyrically, 'Doors To Nowhere' revisits the theme of childhood memories touched upon in earlier tracks such as 'When We Were Younger'. The verses appear to allude to snapshots in time, referencing 'the old Frigidaire' (refrigerator), 'slow dusty trains' and house steps that were 'always cleaned, always brushed' (a common reference point of working-class life in mid-20th century Britain). There's a nostalgic longing for the ordinary everyday experiences of the past as well as the carefree experiences of childhood in the chorus – 'Ran down the hillside/Like we were insane'. But there's also a recognition that these memories may be deceptive – a reflectiveness that's less evident on at least one other track on the album.

'The Visitation' (5:48)

The title track is a prime example of Clarkin's intention to mix things up sonically. It's built on an urgent staccato riff played by guitar and drums. It's a compelling rhythm that plays through the chorus alongside a more conventional melody line. Clarkin revealed on the *Black Country Music Show* in October 2011 that the song's rhythmic complexity made it impossible for members of the band to sing and play at the same time and so it was never recreated live. There's more experimentation in the instrumental break, where lilting piano, bass and acoustic picking give way to a swirling synth passage before the riff returns, first on piano and then guitar.

There's much to admire in this song. It reflects the album's diversity of mood and atmosphere and the shifts in tempo and dynamics are among the most exciting on the record. Ultimately, however, Magnum are all about the melody and, in this respect, 'The Visitation' itself is among the record's slighter compositions.

'Wild Angels' (5:41)

Throughout the reunion years, Clarkin has rejected the suggestion that he ever tries to recreate the formula of the 1980s incarnation of the band, often confessing never to listen to the earlier material. Yet, it's difficult to believe he didn't have *Vigilante* or *Wings Of Heaven* in mind – at least subconsciously – when he was writing 'Wild Angels'. The sense of space created by atmospheric keyboard lines, the deceptively simple yet powerful tune and even the title itself all recall some of the best moments from the band's commercial heyday.

Partly inspired by one of Clarkin's daughters, 'Wild Angels' became one of the album's lead tracks and featured on most dates of the accompanying tour. It was also set to be included (alongside 'Black Skies' and 'Freedom Day') on a proposed remixed promotional single – discussed by Catley in an interview in May 2011 – that never materialised.

'Spin Like A Wheel' (7:21)

This is a bluesy track that builds momentum and emotion through its seven-plus minute duration. It opens with an impassioned Catley vocal over keyboard chords and percussion, the tempo increasing as the drums and guitar drop in at the half-minute mark. This is one of Clarkin's very best melodies. The mournful chords in the verse fit particularly well with the lyric's sentiments of loss and heartache.

A short guitar break follows the first chorus and there's a lovely extended instrumental section incorporating more blues guitar, soulful piano and then a slow build from the rhythm section to another, rockier guitar refrain. At around one and a half minutes, this is almost a song within a song, showcasing Clarkin's guitar abilities but also the technical excellence of the band as a whole. The versatile drumming of James holds the whole thing together, as he alternately builds and slows the pace while maintaining a consistent groove across the song.

Originally called 'Fatal Embrace', detailing a story of unrequited love, the band sensibly retitled it 'Spin Like A Wheel', presumably to reflect its roots-based, blues feel and to avoid it being mistaken for an emo or black metal song. It was also one of the four tunes from *The Visitation* to be chosen for the album tour.

'The Last Frontier' (5:29)

If there's one song that might comfortably have been left off the album, it's 'The Last Frontier'. It is perhaps a little ironic that a song nostalgically celebrating the 'good old days' sounds so dated. In a December 2016 interview for Get Ready to Rock, discussing its selection for *The Valley Of Tears: The Ballads* compilation album, Catley summarised 'The Last Frontier' as a song 'about looking back to your youth in the 50s and how life was then as you perceived it. And where's that England gone that I remember so well?'

The references to recollections of the past are no doubt heartfelt, but they're also rather clunky and clichéd. It's not entirely clear whether Clarkin is depicting an idealised vision of the past (a 'fairytale' as one line puts it) or whether he's reflecting on the effect of time and circumstance on how we remember. It could be both. Either way, it's not among his most insightful lyrics. Musically, too, 'The Last Frontier' ambles along without a great deal of urgency, lacking the emotional delivery of some of the band's more effective slower tracks. The overall sound is much too syrupy and it ends up feeling rather contrived.

'Freedom Day' (6:22)
From the weakest song on the album to perhaps the strongest, 'Freedom Day' is one of the standout tracks of Magnum's reunion period. The song is a call to freedom, a 'paean of praise to self-determination' as one reviewer put it. 'We live in freedom in Europe', Clarkin commented, 'but looking at a lot of South American or African countries, you see oppression, you see people living under the brutal reign of a dictator'. By the time of the album's release in January 2011, the anti-government protests and uprisings known as the Arab Spring were underway, giving the song an added poignancy.

'Freedom Day' encapsulated the variations in harmony and rhythm that Clarkin admitted were a feature of the album, and which led some to identify a return to the more progressive material of the 1970s on *The Visitation*. It begins with Clarkin soloing over atmospheric keyboard chords before a more classically inspired piano melody yields to a yearning Catley vocal. The verse is low-key, almost melancholic and then there's a gradual quickening in tempo before the burst into the euphoric chorus:

Shout for your freedom, yell and they will hear the chorus
Bang on your freedom bell, they wouldn't dare ignore us
Into the flame, out of the earth, nothing shall remain.

It's a simple but powerful chorus that alternates through the rest of the song with the slower, sombre verse and beautiful piano-led sections. 'Freedom Day' is a prime example of the central role Stanway's keyboard sound still played in enhancing the power and impact of the band's songs.

'Mother Nature's Final Dance' (5:04)
Here, Magnum tackle another serious real-world topic: global environmental destruction. Although he claimed not to have been inspired by specific events, in interviews, Clarkin did mention the leaking of toxic red sludge from an aluminium plant in Hungary and the *Deepwater Horizon* oil spill in the Gulf of Mexico, which both took place in 2010. 'It's always a mixture of greed and lack of responsibilities which leads to these kinds of tragedies', he observed in an interview with *Sleaze Roxx* website. The lyrics also hint at some of the preoccupations of earlier albums. There's a particular *Eleventh Hour* vibe to the song's imagery. Lines such as, 'So into the shadows burning/Wide-eyed so young they came/And all but their very soul/Swept into that savage game',

recall both the Rodney Matthews cover of the 1983 album and the lyrics of one of the songs that inspired it, 'Young And Precious Souls'. The words are also rare for Magnum (and most bands) in that no lyrics are repeated in the course of the song.

'Mother Nature's Final Dance' is another track that builds in tempo and intensity. The chorus is driven along by a staccato guitar phrase, allied to urgent drums and bass, and there's another lovely soaring melody.

'Midnight Kings' (4:49)
A possible entry (alongside 'Wild Angels') to Magnum's 'song title Bingo', 'Midnight Kings' is one of The *Visitation*'s more conventional, up-tempo tunes. It opens with a heavy riff, accompanied by unconstrained guitar licks that repeat in the chorus, alternating with slower keyboard passages in the verse. It's an altogether more positive and straightforward song than what precedes it and was possibly sequenced to offset the more serious social and political messages of earlier tracks. There's a tasty Clarkin solo and James is on belting form throughout. The unexpected orchestrated coda also works well. However, in the context of a fairly dense and dark album, this could be considered a rather lightweight, throwaway track.

'Tonight's The Night' (4:53)
'Tonight's The Night' is a surprisingly subdued ending to the album. Its high point is the delightful guitar refrain that opens things up and also forms the basis for the melody in the verse. There's a hint of Jeff Lynne and ELO in the tune and the instrumentation, which is reinforced in the mid-song 'Remember' barbershop vocal section. If the verse is consciously laid-back, the chorus is more conventionally anthemic. It's not exactly a 'big' chorus on par with the 1980s but certainly has many of the ingredients of a latter-day 'lighters in the air' classic. It's possible that the relatively understated approach of songs like 'Tonight's The Night' might have prompted Dome's view of Magnum 'going through the motions' on *The Visitation*. Although hardly experimental, this was another interesting piece that delicately contributed to the evolving sound of the band, rather than blindly replicating an established formula.

Related Tracks
'Eyes Like Fire'
Originally mentioned in previews of the album, 'Eyes Like Fire' was eventually included only as a video on the bonus DVD of the expanded edition. A full audio version appeared on the bonus disc of the next album, *On The Thirteenth Day*. Clarkin reasoned that the song was left off *The Visitation* simply because the band wanted ten songs on this occasion and presumably, this was considered the weakest. While not in the highest echelon of Clarkin compositions, had it been included on *The Visitation* instead of 'The Last Frontier' or 'Midnight Kings', or as an additional track, it certainly wouldn't

have weakened the album. In 2020, the song was revived by the young English rock band THEIA, who released a shorter and snappier version as a single.

On The Thirteenth Day (2012)

Personnel:
Tony Clarkin: guitars and backing vocals
Bob Catley: lead vocals
Mark Stanway: keyboards
Al Barrow: bass and backing vocals
Harry James: drums
Additional musicians:
Choir on 'From Within': Sue Parkes, Dan Clark, Susanna Westwood, Tony
Nicholl, Mark Carlton, Stacey Green, Kay Savannah, Debra K Tonks, Mark Tonks,
Katy Jane G
Dan Clark: brass on 'See How They Fall' (note: this may be a misprint of 'bass')
Produced at M2 Studios, Coven, UK by Tony Clarkin
Engineer: Sheena Sear
Cover artwork: Rodney Matthews
Release date: 21 September 2012 on SPV/Steamhammer
Highest chart places: UK: 43, Germany: 28, Sweden: 29
Running time: 57:35

Magnum's 17th studio album, *On The Thirteenth Day,* arrived in the middle
of one of the most productive periods of the band's career. It was released in
September 2012, just 18 months after *The Visitation* and ten months after the
Evolution compilation, which included two new studio tracks. In an interview
with GTFM Radio, Clarkin summarised the reason for the relatively short
space between releases:

> Our plan [in 2011] was to play a lot of festivals, which didn't happen. We
> found ourselves sitting on our butts. I spoke to everyone, saying, 'let's do the
> album now'. I'd actually got an album well on the way even when we were
> touring *The Visitation.*

Other reports suggested that as many as 12 new songs had already been
completed, presumably including 'The Fall' and 'Do You Know Who You Are?',
which were eventually put on *Evolution.*
On The Thirteenth Day underlined the band's quality control as well as its
prodigious work ethic. It not only contained some of Magnum's finest recent
material but was also probably the most consistent collection of the post-
reunion period. There's not a weak song here and, as with *The Visitation,*
there's enough variety in atmosphere and arrangement to prevent the mid-
album troughs that tended to blight later records.
There's little significant difference in sound or production from the previous
album. Catley and Stanway both considered it one of the band's rockier
albums and there's certainly a heavy vibe on some of the songs akin to
The Visitation. Yet it's also a more immediate collection of songs, with less

experimentation and fewer of the progressive segments that had characterised *The Visitation*. Catley told *The Rocktologist* website that although Clarkin's writing remained 'very varied' and 'eclectic', the songs as a whole were 'a little bit more straightforward than before'.

The Rodney Matthews coverfeatures an evil-looking elf figure in the foreground holding up the storyteller's staff with a scroll emblazoned with the album's title. The *Vigilante* logo is used again, but on this occasion, the letters, draped like bunting above the elf's head, appear to be dripping blood. There's less detail than on most Matthews covers, but we still have a purple *Chase The Dragon* tree with its red fruit on the left and the *Moonking* ship at the top. The lights and colours in the background give the image a fairground vibe, which is continued in the inner sleeve with the Al Barrow-designed lighted 'M' and star, bringing to mind old-fashioned fairground signs.

'All The Dreamers' (7:09)

This extended opener starts well with swathes of atmospheric keyboards à la 'On a Storyteller's Night' and Catley humming a lovely wordless melody, which is then echoed by guitar prior to breaking into a stately mid-paced riff. We're at 1.42 before Catley comes in with the song's opening lines: 'The weekend's started/It sounds like thunder'. The following lines – 'Inside this fairground/Of noise and wonder' – allude to the cover illustration and the wider album imagery. These allusions aside, the lyrics are a fairly straightforward celebration of the Magnum fanbase and concert experience, depicting 'the faithful followers' coming to a gig as Catley described it to Rok Podgrajšek of *The Rocktologist* website.

'All The Dreamers' is a solid enough Magnum opening track, but it doesn't quite justify its seven-minute-plus running time. The middle section is a tad predictable and with little variation in structure or dynamics, it ultimately feels slightly ponderous and repetitive towards the end.

'Blood Red Laughter' (4:40)

'Blood Red Laughter' is one of the album's highlights, a stunning blend of crunchy guitar and lilting piano that includes not one but three great hooks. This is one of many later Magnum songs that sounds good on first listen but only really reveals its depth and complexity on subsequent hearings. Stanway is on particularly fine form here, the subtle keyboard phrases providing additional texture to the verse and a commercial edge to the beefy guitar in the bridge and chorus. It's also blessed with one of Clarkin's very best middle sections, a beautiful mini-ballad making full use of Catley's impassioned vocals and a brilliantly crisp guitar solo.

Lyrically, it may be one of Clarkin's more personal compositions. When quizzed on the song's meaning by GTFM's Andy Fox, Clarkin only revealed that the 'Blood red laughter/Across your face' referred to a girl he'd known who painted lipstick and then 'pushed it across her face'. He wouldn't say any more, encouraging fans to simply read the lyrics. The deluxe CD version of the album included a slightly shorter acoustic take, which underlined the quality of the song.

'Didn't Like You Anyway' (4:33)
The final chords of 'Blood Red Laughter' segue into the equally memorable opening refrain of 'Didn't Like You Anyway'. The guitar and synthesised cello combine to create a sharp staccato riff that shapes the track. The string sound isn't out of place or inauthentic, but it would be interesting to know whether the incorporation of real strings, as on previous albums, might have lifted the song to another level. Nonetheless, this is a richly melodic track that maintains the high quality of the album's first phase.

'Didn't Like You Anyway' is one of two songs on the album 'inspired' by the global financial crisis of 2007-2008 and its ramifications. Clarkin told Andy Fox that the song was specifically 'stirred' by the role of bankers and the banking crisis, although it could also refer to politicians and, indeed, anyone you didn't like. The focus on banking is evident in lines like 'I hear you call that dealing/That's not the word I'd use/'Cause some might call it stealing/ No pretence, that's just abuse' and the song's opening references to 'skilful calculation', 'sly manipulation' and 'money and greed'.

'On The Thirteenth Day' (5:35)
'Didn't Like You Anyway' merges into the title track, a pacey and dynamic song reminiscent of the FM/Polydor era of the band and with a guitar riff suggestive of the previous album's 'Doors To Nowhere'. There's a vague fantasy theme in the title and the lyrics. The song originally referred to 'the Twelfth Day', but this was changed because the phrase was considered too common in popular culture and was specifically linked to Christmas. The number thirteen was chosen instead due to its darker, more ominous associations that tied in with the generalised apocalyptic sentiments of the lyrics. It was also presumably chosen because the word scanned better.

Although there's no obvious conceptual unity between the songs, 'Blood Red Laughter', 'Didn't Like You Anyway' and 'On The Thirteenth Day' are arranged as a connected suite of tunes with no gaps between them. It's a device that the band had used before – most notably on *Kingdom Of Madness* – and it works particularly well here. It's helped by the sheer quality of these three tracks, adding a breathless intensity that establishes this as the best opening section of a Magnum album since the 1980s. 'On The Thirteenth Day' is a strangely neglected track. It would have been a more effective album opener than 'All The Dreamers' and might easily have replaced that song on tour.

'So Let It Rain' (4:50)
'So Let It Rain' is the most overtly commercial Magnum track since the 1990s. With keyboards prominent in the mix, layers of backing vocals and a catchy

singalong chorus, this is the closest Clarkin has come to emulating the pop-rock textures of songs like 'Start Talking Love' and 'It Must Have Been Love'. Catley's raspier vocals are the main indication that this is a 2012 rather than a 1988 vintage. The song might seem out of place amongst the album's heavier material, but the sequencing works well and lyrically, it fits with some of the more reflective tracks. The song was released as a single, though only as a CD and only in Germany. It included a slightly truncated radio edit and a live version of 'Wild Angels', recorded in Aschaffenburg.

'Dance Of The Black Tattoo' (5:16)

Following on from one of the album's lighter moments, we have probably the heaviest track Magnum have ever released. 'Dance Of The Black Tattoo' is a *tour de force* that underlines the band's presence at the intersection of melodic rock, classic rock and heavy metal as well as its ability to mix power and grace in a single song. Incorporating modern metal touches, the guitars are downtuned and the riffs are raw and relentless. Yet, subtleties abound in Stanway's fabulous keyboard fills, James' pinpoint drum work and Barrow's sturdy bass playing. Barrow admitted that he loved playing the song live because it gave him the opportunity to 'just sit in the groove and supply the big rumble'. This is a classic ensemble performance from the band, with everyone at the top of their game.

It's also a brilliantly constructed track, full of contrasts and surprises, such as the fairground waltz at the end that once again alludes to the cover theme. It's a song that pushes the band beyond its comfort zone and yet still manages to sound unmistakably 'Magnum'.

'Dance Of The Black Tattoo' is this album's representative anti-war track. The 'Black Tattoo' references the drum tattoo accompanying troops as they march to battle. But there's a deeper and more personal meaning aligned with the lyrics of the chorus in particular. Clarkin:

Sometimes, soldiers don't talk about the horrors they see ... They wouldn't even write it in a diary. Like, 'The diary's empty' in other words... The horrors they see in war – they can't speak about it, couldn't even write it in a diary.

This was true of Clarkin's own father, who had never spoken about his wartime experiences.

'Shadow Town' (5:57)

Although it may seem an upbeat, even joyful song on the surface, 'Shadow Town' is a rumination on the impact of the global depression on local businesses and communities. Clarkin observed that it reflected the fortunes of his own hometown, Lichfield, in the West Midlands of England: 'It's a lovely small town and in the last two or three years, all the shops have just shut down and it's becoming dead'. The impact of the internet and large shopping centres had thus destroyed town centres, creating 'shadow towns' where 'life's much harder to keep on living'.

Numerous reviews pointed to the Springsteen-esque quality of the song. There are certainly similarities in the instrumentation and vocal delivery, although these influences are accommodated without resorting to pastiche. 'Shadow Town' was a particular favourite of Catley. He felt it could become a popular live song, although, ultimately, it wasn't one of the four album cuts chosen for the subsequent tour. Special note should be made of the close harmonies through the verse and chorus, which add an extra melodic texture to the song. 'Shadow Town' is also given the acoustic treatment on the deluxe CD and what a great version it is too; in fact, it's one of the highlights of the whole package.

'Putting Things In Place' (4:41)

The tempo drops a notch for one of the best ballads in the Magnum repertoire. 'Putting Things In Place' is fairly straightforward in structure and sound. It's built on Stanway's achingly beautiful piano and luscious keyboard soundscapes, which the rest of the band add to in typical power ballad style as the song builds momentum. Yet there's also restraint and subtlety in the performance and the production. Dripping in emotion from the start, Catley's vocal is allowed to carry the song. There's a recognition that the core of the track is in the careful undulating path of the melody and so Clarkin avoids drowning this out or including the type of overwrought guitar solo that had become a cliché in rock and metal ballads.

The lyrics underline the emotional intricacy of the song. Put simply, as Catley did in one interview at the time, it's 'about loss and not knowing what to do, so you just tidy up'. But beyond that, the lyrics touch on the connections between losing someone you love, memory and the ordinary routines of daily life, such as arranging one's clothes and hair. It's these mundane features of living that cause the subject of the song to break down and scream out loud and so she 'Puts things in place/Just to get by'.

'Putting Things In Place', Catley told the *Express and Star* newspaper in October 2012:

> I love too much to sing. It nearly made it onto the setlist, but we had a rethink. I've got to sing it, don't forget and you know how upset I get... maybe not a good idea for Bob to be blarting [crying] his eyes out. It's very personal... We've all had loss in our families and our lives, and so I'm kind of glad we're not doing it.

'Broken Promises' (4:41)

A song detailing relationship breakdowns, 'Broken Promises' is a solid track in the classic rock mould. The opening guitar refrain echoes Blue Öyster Cult's 'Don't Fear The Reaper' and elsewhere, there are hints of Deep

Purple. There's an unusually unrestrained Clarkin guitar solo and another tight performance by the band's rhythm section. The chorus is particularly effective, lifting an otherwise fairly standard album track. It does offer another example of Magnum's ability to write heavier material, but it hardly breaks new ground in the way 'Dance Of The Black Tattoo' does. Such is the quality of the album that 'Broken Promises' is probably the least essential track. But it's still well beyond what most hard rock bands – veteran or otherwise – were producing at the time.

'See How They Fall' (4:56)

Another standout track, 'See How They Fall' is based around a martial-style riff that harks back to some of the Jet-era material. The verse and chorus are dominated by a chugging guitar groove, which drives the song forward. Keyboards and guitar blend perfectly in signature Magnum fashion and the lyrics are simple but neatly constructed. The verse, 'Wake me if I'm asleep/ Leave me if it's still dawn/Save me if I'm too deep/Cool me if I'm too warm', works especially well. This is up there with the very best of the rockier post-2002 tracks. It was played throughout the 'On The Thirteenth Day' tour, occasionally as an encore.

'From Within' (4:42)

'From Within' is another fairly subdued closing track with a commercial sensibility and imaginative use of backing vocals. It begins in a mundane fashion lyrically and sonically, but the chord change into the bridge is the turning point, ushering in a lovely, rousing melody that buries itself firmly into the brain on repeated listens. It ends with a mass singalong from a 'choir' of friends and well-wishers. The sentiments are hardly original – 'From within you can run/No hill you can't climb' – and fit a common Clarkin motif of having faith in yourself despite life's obstacles. Ultimately, however, 'From Within' is a fitting finale to perhaps the most consistent and diverse of the post-reunion albums.

Escape From The Shadow Garden (2014)

Personnel:
Tony Clarkin: guitars
Bob Catley: vocals
Mark Stanway: keyboards
Al Barrow: bass, backing vocals
Harry James: drums
Produced at: M2 Studios, Coven, UK by Tony Clarkin
Engineer: Sheena Sear
Release date: 19 March 2014 in Scandinavia, 21 March in Germany, Austria and
Switzerland, 24 March in the rest of Europe, 1 April in US and Canada on SPV/
Steamhammer
Cover design: Rodney Matthews
Highest chart places: UK: 38, Germany: 14, Sweden: 19
Running time: 62.41

Escape From The Shadow Garden was Magnum's 18th album and continued
the band's post-reformation run of success. For the first time since 1992's
Sleepwalking, Magnum made the UK Top 40 album charts and reached the
Top 20 in both Germany and Sweden. With the same line-up as the previous
three albums, and recorded in the same studio as the previous five, it
emphasised the band's stability and consistency.

Although incorporating the usual mixture of ballads and more melodic
tracks, it also continued (and perhaps enhanced) the heavier sound of *On The
Thirteenth Day*. Al Barrow claimed that the darker and heavier tone of some
of the material may have been down to the members (including Clarkin)
listening to bands such as German industrial metallers Rammstein during the
previous tour. Catley also recognised that this collection of songs demanded a
different vocal performance. He adopted a grittier delivery that seemed more
in tune with the harder material and darker themes.

The Rodney Matthews cover likewise drew on recurrent characters and
themes. At the centre of the picture is the storyteller sitting, despondent, at
the foot of a grey tree (recalling *Chase The Dragon*), with a skull-like face
on the trunk. Branches akin to claws are sprouting from the trunk, serpents
appear from the top and the elf from *On The Thirteenth Day* is peering out
from behind the tree. Strange purple fruit in the shape of question marks
are attached to the branches and hands point in various directions, from
the 'Escape from The Shadow Garden' sign as well as from the desolate
landscape. The barren background brings to mind both *The Eleventh Hour*
and, in the citadel visible on the right-hand side and the dragonfly on the
left, *Chase The Dragon*. There are also clear references to the *Vigilante*,
Sleepwalking and *Princess Alice* covers, among others. What it all means
is impossible for anyone apart from Clarkin and Matthews to know, but it
seems to touch on some of the album's more serious themes, such as feeling

trapped and making life-changing decisions. The cover also features the return of the *On A Storyteller's Night* logo, in gold and purple, for the first time since 1985.

'Live 'Til You Die' (6:36)

A typical up-tempo tune to open the album. Ominous orchestrated synths mixed with an urgent keyboard melody fill the first 35 seconds and then the guitar riff comes in. It's another great riff from Clarkin, although it's impossible to deny the similarity to one of the NWOBHM's showpiece tunes: Saxon's '747 (Strangers In The Night)'. Nonetheless, the prominent keyboard flourishes and crunching chorus take the song somewhere else entirely. The chorus, in particular, with its galloping rhythm, demonstrates Clarkin's ability to execute invigorating and punchy hard rock tunes.

The title came from an old man whom Clarkin saw in Lichfield (his hometown) screaming at a girl: 'You're going to live 'til you die'. Less a case of stating the obvious than a call to make the most of each day, the title doesn't necessarily fit with the darker fantasy imagery of the lyrics, which bring to mind earlier albums like *The Eleventh Hour*. 'Sacred the one orphaned child', Catley sings in the chorus, 'Destined to collide/Always cast aside'. The lyrics also allude to both the album title and cover image; 'Gold and purple treasures in your hand' hints at the colour scheme, while later in the second verse, Catley sings about the starlight falling on 'the shadow garden', from which 'there's no escape'. In interviews at the time, Catley talked about the 'Shadow Garden' concept and title only in vague terms: 'I guess we all have our own shadow gardens in our life', he told the *Myglobalmind* webzine, 'somewhere we can escape to when we are in a place we don't want to be'. He then qualified this by saying that the title 'is really whatever you make of it'. That's cleared that up, then.

'Unwritten Sacrifice' (5:28)

The latest in what was by now a long list of war-themed songs, 'Unwritten Sacrifice' focuses on the topic of the unknown soldier or unknown warrior. Heartfelt and emotional, if a little clunky in places, Clarkin's words dwell on the familiar theme of the horrors of war through the case of those combatants (particularly during the First World War) who were left unidentified and whose graves were initially marked with simple rough crosses: 'What was his name? Who were his friends? Give him his self-respect'.

Musically, this is another track that successfully blends heavy guitars and keyboard melody. A dramatic synth opening provides the emotional setting for a crunching Clarkin riff and we're soon onto the powerful wall-of-sound chorus, powered by James' driving drums and augmented cleverly towards the end by choral-style backing vocals. This is nothing new or out of the ordinary for Magnum in terms of subject matter and music, but it's done so effectively here and with such enthusiasm that you can't help but be impressed.

'Falling For The Big Plan' (5:59)

'Unwritten Sacrifice' segues into the third strong song in a row, 'Falling For The Big Plan'. Another of Stanway's soft synth openings leads into lilting piano chords and vocals, which gain momentum with the gradual introduction of drums and guitar. The melody in the chorus is sublime, one of Clarkin's most memorable for some time. There's also a fabulous middle-eight that gives the song its title, followed by a lovely bluesy guitar interlude and a nice extended rock ending.

Once again, the lyrics hint at the fantasy imagery often associated with the band, but the song's meaning seems to be more down to earth. According to Catley, it's about a young girl stuck in a rut and hemmed in by the assumptions of authority figures – teachers, employers and so on. Her 'heading for the border' communicates the need to escape to a new life, echoing the album title and cover. There's also a reference to *The Wizard Of Oz* – 'You're falling for the tin man/Who survives the double feature' – which may hint at the lack of compassion shown by those controlling the girl's old life but also, according to Clarkin, linked to the broader issue of trusting authority figures.

The first three songs all featured prominently in the *Escape From The Shadow Garden* tour and were included on the subsequent live album.

'Crying In The Rain' (5:45)

Four tracks in, the first dip in quality comes with this fairly standard hard rock song. It's not at all bad; the production is great, Catley's voice soars and it's a solid melody. It's perfectly enjoyable and doubtless would have gone down well live. But it just sounds a little too much like any decent hard rock band of the previous four decades. The lyrics are also fairly straightforward 'girl gone bad' stuff, which fails to leave an impression. Catley was doubtless right that it would have made a good single were the band still releasing them. But there is more imaginative music and better representations of the current sound on the album than this.

'Too Many Clowns' (4:36)

A rock 'n' roll song with a twist. Clarkin and Catley had dabbled with rock 'n' roll influences before; on *Rock Art,* for instance, and during the Hard Rain era. But this is no straightforward 1950s replica. For a start, it's heavy as hell, possibly the heaviest track on the album. After a brief infusion of keyboards, guitar and drums open things up, Clarkin's guitar refrain kicks in, propelling the song along. Then, just as it seems to be hitting its groove, the juggernaut riff gives way to a proggy, psych-drenched interlude. 'Look now the circus is here/Too many clowns', Catley whispers and then there's another gear shift to a catchy chorus layered with guitar and keyboards. It's inventive stuff, with Clarkin's guitar work particularly prominent.

'Too Many Clowns' is a fairly unambiguous attack on politicians who crave to be elected but then offer little support or compassion for those in society in greatest need. Although it could be interpreted as targeting uncaring politicians in general, the main focus seemed to be closer to home: 'the clowns who run the country at the moment', as Catley put it in one interview at the time. The chorus particularly draws attention to the plight of the homeless, pensioners and single mothers.

'Midnight Angel' (7:18)
Possibly because of its unusual lyrical content (for Magnum, at least), this song received a lot of attention when the album was released. It is one of the album's 'mini-epics', a story song (inspired by Christine Keeler and the Profumo affair) telling the tale of a young South American girl who falls into sex work, gets caught up with a famous politician and is then murdered to ensure her silence. It certainly demonstrates the broadening of Clarkin's lyrical preoccupations, even if it's more heavy-handed than some of his other efforts.

Musically, it's based on a fairly simple chord progression through the verse, with the line, 'Have you seen the midnight angel?', opening each stanza. There's a suggestion, here, of the evocative simplicity of 'Les Morts Dansant', but whereas that track had a feel that allowed the verses to swing, 'Midnight Angel' doesn't quite flow and ultimately ends up rather turgid. Catley's raspy delivery misses the mark on this one, too; the emotional resonance he's clearly aiming at is never quite convincing. Stanway's accompanying keyboard sound is also oddly jarring and sounds quite dated. The song is almost saved by a typically melodic up-tempo chorus, but ultimately, this is one of the few epics in the Magnum catalogue that just doesn't come off.

'The Art Of Compromise' (5:01)
An odd title, perhaps from a songwriter who, in his singer's words, 'doesn't do compromise', this song is about the give and take of relationships. Stanway is given a rare opportunity to shine. There's a beautiful piano introduction and chiming chords that play off against the guitar in the chorus. The keyboards also feature heavily in the down-tempo middle eight that launches into a short but tasteful Clarkin guitar solo.

This is the sort of mellifluous track that Clarkin had become incredibly adept at producing by this point in the band's career. It isn't a masterpiece by any stretch of the imagination but it is high-quality, well-structured and meaningful melodic rock. It is also one of a number of the songs on *Escape From The Shadow Garden* that, consciously or unconsciously, recall earlier lyrical motifs. The lines, 'Never stumble, never fall, Don't you know you've got it all', certainly reminded this listener of similar sentiments in 'When The World Comes Down', one of the band's best-loved songs.

'Don't Fall Asleep' (5:59)
The first outright ballad on the album, 'Don't Fall Asleep', is another track that tips its hat to some of the band's 1980s classics. The imagery in the

lines, 'Don't fall asleep and fear the raging storm/Just let your magic lantern burn', brings to mind 'On A Storyteller's Night'. Equally, the song's message of supporting those who need it during difficult times of their life echoes the theme as well as specific lines in 'When The World Comes Down'.

We're in genuine power ballad territory here. Building from a slow, plaintive Catley vocal over the top of gentle keyboard chords (that sound a little too similar to Styx's 'Babe' for my liking), the song comes to life in the sweeping, majestic chorus. Although not a great deal happens in the course of the song, it never drags. The middle eight is lovely and while the keyboard passage that follows simply repeats the main tune, it works perfectly.

Given the sheer number of ballads in Magnum's repertoire, it's perhaps not surprising that 'Don't Fall Asleep' is overlooked. Indeed, it often seems overshadowed on the album itself by the epic closer, 'The Valley Of Tears'. But it's a corking tune that makes good use of the instrumental prowess of Stanway on an album where the keyboards are generally marginalised.

'Wisdom's Had Its Day' (4:44)
Starting off with Catley's voice accompanied by melancholic minor key piano, the song builds into a slow, menacing shuffle. The chorus, built on a call and response between the vocals and keyboard melody, is dramatic (or bombastic, depending on your viewpoint) in typical Magnum style. The second chorus leads into a fine middle-eight starring Catley at his emotional best, which then drops into a soft piano passage. The chorus returns with layered harmony vocals, with a marching drum beat adding to the rhythmic tension. The song comes full circle at the end, with Catley repeating the two lines that started the song – 'We're hopelessly confused/Wisdom's had its day' – over Stanway's piano.

A hidden gem in the Magnum catalogue, 'Wisdom's Had Its Day' demonstrates Clarkin's compositional skill as well as his ear for the less obvious melody line. It was probably too downbeat and complex to play live, but it provided additional evidence that the band were always capable of more than your average melodic rock act.

'Burning River' (4:43)
This is another fairly straightforward melodic rock track, but the Magnum imprint is all over this one. In tempo and feel, it's a close cousin of 'Hanging Tree' from the *Goodnight LA* sessions. The infectious 1980s-sounding guitar hook drives the song along, although it's again offset by vaguely fantastical lyrics that probably have a deeper meaning. Some of Clarkin's most interesting wordplay on the album involves him dabbling with mythical, other-worldly imagery: 'And your fire will be turned to ice/All your horses returned to mice/By a killer lagoon/On the night of the wayward moon'. The meaning is less important here than the successful marriage of imagery and music.

'Burning River' is another half-buried semi-classic. It varies the tempo of the album cleverly, helping it to avoid the mid-paced flatness from which some later Magnum albums suffer.

'The Valley Of Tears' (6:39)

And so, to the closing epic. Of the later Magnum ballads, this one seems to be particularly popular. It's certainly very well constructed. It has a slow build, a soaring chorus and is expertly played. And it's another impressive performance by Catley, throwing the emotional kitchen sink at an evocative set of lyrics that once again recall the 'When The World Comes Down' narrative of resilience under pressure and making the most of what you have. Yet, ultimately, it's a little too overblown and overlong. There's not the restraint and subtlety evident in the band's more successful latter-day ballads and the melody is simply not as powerful as the song it most resembles in the catalogue: 'Face In the Crowd' from *Into The Valley Of The Moonking*.

Sacred Blood 'Divine' Lies (2016)

Personnel:
Tony Clarkin: guitars and backing vocals
Bob Catley: lead vocals
Mark Stanway: keyboards
Al Barrow: bass and backing vocals
Harry James: drums
Produced at M2 Studios, Coven, by Tony Clarkin
Engineer: Sheena Sear
Release date: 26 February 2016 on SPV/Steamhammer
Cover Illustration: Rodney Matthews
Highest chart places: UK: 31, Germany: 20, Sweden: 23
Running time: 54:21

Clarkin began working on Magnum's 19th album around March 2014, just after the release of its predecessor, *Escape From The Shadow Garden*. He was writing during and after the European tour in April and May and amassed something in the region of 25 songs that were whittled down to 16, then to 13 and finally to the ten that made the album, with the three leftover tracks included as bonuses on the digipack DVD.

There was no major change in sound or production, but the band again emphasised the increasing heaviness of the material. The press release identified Clarkin's 'awesome riffing and hard driving lead guitar licks' as 'the all-important substructure' to the material on the album. As Clarkin was quoted as saying:

I've always been into rock numbers. But it isn't necessarily that easy to write really good rock material. It's much more simple to compose a ballad. But that dynamic pace suits Magnum perfectly.

Although the production had been moving this way for a few albums, the guitars are both more prominent and have a harder edge than on previous outings, with the keyboards a little more marginal to the overall sound.

While it's a solid album, with four or five excellent tracks, *Sacred Blood 'Divine' Lies* doesn't quite keep up the quality of the three albums that preceded it. It's hardly possible to say that it halted the band's late-career momentum – the UK chart position of number 31 was the highest since 1992 – but it's the first album since *Into The Valley Of The Moonking* where some of the material has sounded jaded and lacking in inspiration.

Matthews' sleeve featured a futurist alien-type villain on a throne, with gold and riches at his feet, surrounded by ghostly images of the children from *The Eleventh Hour* sleeve. He's addressing the schoolboy and his dog from the *Into The Valley Of The Moonking* cover. The back cover has a desert setting with buildings and spires in the distance, echoing various elements of earlier album covers, particularly *Chase The Dragon*. As always, the detail

121

in the illustration is impressive, especially as Matthews was up against time to complete it as he had been for *On A Storyteller's Night*. However, while it's excellently realised, it's not the most distinctive or original of Magnum covers. It's also worth noting that the inverted commas added to the word 'divine' in the title arose because Matthews (a practising Christian) disliked the title and insisted, according to his website, that there was 'no such thing as divine lies'.

'Sacred Blood 'Divine' Lies' (6:41)
This was a rare Clarkin composition that started as a poem and to which the music was later added. An allegory about political or spiritual leaders who 'behave like gods' and 'believe that they are in touch with the divine', given its origin, it's not surprising that it's one of the wordier lyrics in the band's catalogue. The guitarist told the *Metal Kaoz* website in March 2016 that he kept singing the words against a riff he'd been working on in the studio and that that became the chorus.

Based on a chunky, serpentine riff, it's also one of Magnum's heavier songs and an indication of the increasing emphasis on building material around the lead guitar. Buoyed by a tight rhythm section, aside from the short middle eight, there's barely any let-up in the song's sludgy groove. Catley's raspy singing also suits the song perfectly. At not far off seven minutes, it's longer than it needs to be but a solid statement of intent nonetheless.

'Crazy Old Mothers' (5:48)
Like 'Sacred Blood', this is firmly in 1970s rock territory in places, particularly in the chorus with its insistent mid-paced groove. There is more light and shade here, though, with Stanway's piano taking on the introductory melody and a number of turns of mood and tempo to keep things interesting. Band members have given a couple of, not necessarily incompatible, versions of the song's meaning. On *Metal Kaoz*, Clarkin noted that the inspiration came from a reunion with bandmates in one of his 1960s groups, one of whom regretted giving up playing when he did. This fits with lines such as, 'You walk in the shadows/You gave in too soon'. He provided more detail at the time of the release of the promo video for the song, saying it was 'about working in a job you hate when you had such big plans for yourself, but you were too scared to take a chance and follow them through'. Catley, meanwhile, has suggested that the song should be seen as a tribute to Magnum's longest-standing fans. He told *NI Rocks* in May 2016 that it was inspired by a group of older fans during the previous tour getting drunk, singing and behaving outrageously. It underlines the role of music in keeping people in touch with their youth: 'Don't act your age and never grow up. Just keep young in your head'.

'Gypsy Queen' (4:29)
One could be forgiven for thinking Clarkin was listening to a lot of 1970s and 1980s hard rock while writing the album. Another track where the riff

is king, this one has more than a passing musical and lyrical resemblance to Deep Purple in its pomp. The extended bluesy solo from 2.44 to 3.28 is pure Ritchie Blackmore. The slow, atmospheric section at the beginning and in the verses was not in the original version but was introduced by Clarkin as he refined the track.

The lyric was inspired by a visit to St. Petersburg back in 1992, where the band were playing a festival. Clarkin visited Palace Square during the day and recalls it being a magical place, vowing to write a song about it one day. In particular, he noticed a number of bedraggled girls wandering around the square and let his imagination run wild, visualising one of the girls as a gypsy queen 'with gold and ribbons in her hair'. The band liked the song but apparently couldn't get it to work in rehearsal, so it didn't feature on the *Sacred Blood* tour.

'Princess In Rags (The Cult)' (5:27)
This is another track built around a heavy and dynamic guitar riff. It is a fairly conventionally structured Magnum song in that the quieter, keyboard-infused verse gives way to the hard-hitting anthemic chorus. It includes an unusually fast, almost shredding Clarkin guitar solo, from 3.40. A song about children getting caught up in cults, the inclusion of the subtitle may be to distinguish it from American singer-songwriter Gene Pitney's 1965 hit.

'Your Dreams Won't Die' (5:25)
A song about loss, memory and meaning, 'Your Dreams Won't Die' is a simple but deeply poignant number. Clarkin certainly felt strongly about the track. 'To me', he was quoted as saying, 'the title and lyrics have an almost religious depth'. It tapped into the common idea that a person isn't forgotten if their name stays in the memory. Musically, it's carefully constructed to provoke an emotional response, with chiming keyboards and mournful strings to the fore. Indeed, according to the press release, the track was 'based on a cascading chord sequence, reflecting... [its] philosophical message'. The song emerged as one of the band's popular latter-day ballads, staying in the live set for the next couple of tours.

'Afraid Of The Night' (4:32)
This is another track that seems to channel the spirit of classic rock, this time in relation to the writing of the late Ronnie James Dio, whom Catley frequently identified as one of his favourite singers. While it's another song based on a powerful guitar stomp, it also includes a number of time changes and prog rock touches, such as the dream-like bridge from 2.33-3.13 that morphs into a brief anthemic guitar refrain. This is so good that it might have been developed further to give the track added depth. Speaking to Andy Fox of GTFM Radio in March 2016, Catley recalled that the band nearly forgot about 'Afraid Of The Night' when planning the tracklisting for the album

before resurrecting the backing tracks, deciding it was strong enough to be included and adding vocals.

'A Forgotten Conversation' (4:56)
Most post-reunion Magnum albums have one or two gems buried in the middle of the record. 'A Forgotten Conversation' is *Sacred Blood*'s 'Wisdom's Had Its Day', a carefully conceived earworm that rewards repeated listening. Opening with plaintive keyboard chords, not unlike 'Putting Things In Place' from *On The Thirteenth Day*, it later shifts into a lively yet brooding piano and guitar refrain with pounding drums and a few gorgeous melodic touches. There's nothing bombastic or over-complex here, but it works a treat; the chorus, with its repeated 'the room was empty' lines, could have come from the *Wings Of Heaven* sessions.

'Quiet Rhapsody' (5:40)
Another song built around a heavy chugging guitar riff, this takes a bit of time to get going. It's fairly typical of the slightly edgy melodic hard rock tunes Clarkin was still able to roll out four decades into the band's career. As on much of the album, there's a genuine groove to the music, aided by James' tight drumming. Despite this, it's one of the least memorable tracks on the album and, as in other cases, it's at least a minute and a half too long.

'Twelve Men Wise And Just' (6:18)
On an album dominated (unusually for Magnum) by relatively straightforward hard rock songs, the penultimate track offers a contrast with a range of subtle touches and musical variation. This is a track that really builds, from Stanway's lyrical piano opening to the more conventional guitar stomp of the verse and ascending pre-chorus. At the heart of the song, however, is a sweeping, majestic chorus underpinned by galloping bass and a beautiful synth counter melody and piano fill. The production makes the whole thing sound big and bold, echoing some of Clarkin's most inspired writing of the band's first incarnation. It may not be as heavy as the majority of the album, but 'Twelve Men Wise And Just' is the standout track, both intricate and intense in the best Magnum tradition.

'Don't Cry Baby' (5:05)
A fairly typical melancholic Magnum album closer, this was one of Clarkin's favourite songs at the time of its release. There's a lovely wistful melody and the programmed drums, which the band decided to keep from the demo because they sounded so good, give the recording a slightly nostalgic, spacey 1980s vibe. This is reinforced by the moody middle eight at 2.36 and Clarkin's expressive bluesy guitar break that leads into the fade-out. Although it isn't exactly consistent with the mood of the rest of the album, 'Don't Cry Baby' is another highlight.

Related Tracks

For the first time, the band decided to release the songs that didn't quite make the cut as bonus tracks. Clarkin normally took the view that the songs that were shelved couldn't have been up to standard. On this occasion, while the additional songs weren't included because they disrupted the flow of the main album, he felt they were good enough to be heard.

'Phantom Of Paradise Circus' (5:54)

There's plenty of variation in this snaking track that incorporates southern rock riffs, keyboard themes and another galloping chorus with a soaring melody line. It has all the makings of a Magnum epic but ultimately doesn't quite deliver. Nonetheless, it's a solid enough song with plenty going on that really grows with repeated listens.

'Don't Grow Up' (4:47)

This is a high-intensity guitar rock track in keeping with the tone of the main album. But it's the least exciting of the bonus tracks and it's not hard to see why it didn't make the final album cut.

'No God Or Saviour' (5:53)

The gentle, lilting verse alone, with its echo of Bon Jovi's 'Wanted Dead Or Alive', is enough to have made this worthy of inclusion on the main album. But it's made more interesting still by combining it with the harsher, slow, staccato guitar chug in the chorus. Taken together, it's a particularly memorable track, although the absence of a solo where it appears to be needed at 4.00 suggests it might not have been properly finished.

Lost On The Road To Eternity (2018)

Personnel:

Tony Clarkin: guitar

Bob Catley: vocals

Rick Benton: keyboards

Al Barrow: bass guitar

Lee Morris: drums

Additional Musicians:

Wolf Kerscheck Orchestra: arranged and conducted by Wolf Kerscheck

Tobias Sammet: additional vocals on 'Lost On The Road To Eternity'

Lee Small: additional vocals on 'King Of The World' and 'Without Love'

Lee Small, Liam Docherty and Louis Coupe: additional vocals on 'Ya Wanna Be Someone'

Dan Clark: additional bass on 'Without Love' and 'King Of The World'

Produced at M2 Studios, Coven, by Tony Clarkin

Engineer: Sheena Sear

Release date: 19 January 2018 on SPV/Steamhammer

Cover Illustration: Rodney Matthews

Highest chart places: UK: 15, Germany: 8, Sweden: 23

Running time: 66:53

Two significant line-up changes took place before the release of Magnum's 20th album in January 2018. In December 2016, midway through the *Sacred Blood 'Divine' Lies* winter tour, Mark Stanway left the band. The precise reasons that prompted him to pack his bags and leave immediately are not entirely clear and, anyway, probably not particularly important. Stanway announced in a statement that he'd departed due to 'irrevocable circumstances'; he later told the *Outsider Rock* website that 'there are 36 years' worth of small reasons which accumulated and came to a head which basically made my decision/mind up for me'. He also noted that tensions with other members of the band increased when his autobiography *Close To The Mark* was published in 2015.

In the short term, the band needed a keyboard player to complete the tour. They recruited session musician Rick Benton, who had worked with Mark Stuart at M2 Studios and had considerable experience as a musical director for artists, production companies and studios. Benton bonded so well with the band, musically and personally, that he was made a full member just over a month later, in January 2017.

Meanwhile, in the summer of 2017, the band made the reluctant decision to let drummer Harry James go. It was becoming increasingly difficult to coordinate James' Magnum work with that of his other bands, Thunder and Snakecharmer. In his place came Lee Morris, an experienced drummer who had played with Birmingham band Marshall Law from the late 1980s and then with pioneering gothic metallers Paradise Lost between 1995 and 2004. Both

Al Barrow and Annie Minion, Catley's personal manager, recommended Morris and, after watching him play online, the band hired him without an audition.

Whether or not it was due to the addition of this new blood, *Lost On The Road To Eternity* is a vital and inspired recording. The band's longest studio album to date, it incorporates a sprinkling of sparky, commercial tunes, a couple of bombastic epics and a fully orchestrated title track complete with a guest co-vocalist. There's a shift away from the heavier material of the previous few albums towards a more balanced approach, with keyboards front and centre on a number of compositions. While it may not quite represent a late-career magnum opus, *Lost On The Road To Eternity* certainly deserves to be considered alongside *Brand New Morning, Princess Alice And The Broken Arrow, On The Thirteenth Day* and *Escape From The Shadow Garden* as among the finest of Magnum's reunion collections.

Increased media interest in the new record led to the lead track 'Without Love' being selected for the BBC Radio 2 playlist in January 2018. An appearance on the Musician's Circle session of Radio 2's Michael Ball show followed, where the band (augmented by backing vocalists Lee Small and Rebecca Downes) played acoustic versions of 'Without Love' and a cover of Bob Dylan's 'Knocking On Heaven's Door'. This all contributed to the highest chart placings in decades throughout much of Europe, with Top Ten appearances in Germany (8) and Switzerland (9) and number 15 in the UK. It also heralded the band's biggest UK and European tour for years, a 42-date extravaganza taking in ten countries across February, March and April 2018.

The cover illustration by Rodney Matthews once again includes the schoolboy in striped uniform with his dog. This time, he was depicted alongside a range of characters from children's literature, mainly from Lewis Carroll's *Alice In Wonderland* and *The Wizard Of Oz,* but also Robin Hood, Sherlock Holmes and an angel holding the sword of chaos to the left with the grim reaper (wearing a Micky Mouse badge) to the right. It's one of Matthews' most detailed and compelling album sleeves: the artist himself considered it his best Magnum cover since *On A Storyteller's Night*. He also revealed on his website that Clarkin's initial idea for the sleeve was 'a bloke crucified to a wind turbine', an admittedly 'controversial' concept that was quickly rejected.

'Peaches And Cream' (4:54)

This is a great album opener. At heart, it's a pretty up-front, foot-to-the-floor rocker, full of verve and with a solid meat and potatoes riff. Yet, as is frequently true of Magnum, it also contains a wealth of subtle twists and surprises. What's immediately evident is that the keyboards have been pushed higher up the mix than on the previous few albums. While this is a guitar-led song, Benton is involved throughout, contributing piano fills and runs, bracing chords in the middle eight and doubling up the guitar riff with organ in the chorus. This all adds significantly to the flavour of what might otherwise have been a fairly one-dimensional track. Thematically, it seems to be a simple play on the fairly antiquated idiom chosen for the title – the notion that life is relatively easy. Clarkin is keen to emphasise the struggles and difficulties of people's life experiences – that in reality, there's 'no happy ending' and 'no fairy tale' – and that success is only achieved through considerable hard work.

'Show Me Your Hands' (5:45)

Speaking to the *Outsider Rock* website a couple of months prior to the release of the album, Benton outlined the three main ways in which keyboards are used in Magnum songs. First, they can be utilised to lock into a groove and back up the guitar rhythms; second, they might be employed to create a 'mood' or a 'scene' for the song; and third, there might be more 'virtuosic' keyboard performances, involving complex piano parts, string arrangements and so on. 'Show Me Your Hands' is a prime example of the latter, with the keyboard operating as a lead instrument and taking on the main riffs and solos. Indeed, it's fair to say that even this early into his debut album with the band, Benton is beginning to develop a characteristic style, as highlighted by a couple of dazzling breaks between 3.13-3.19 and 3.33-3.49 (the second more reminiscent of Bailey than Stanway).

Another Magnum song celebrating the fans and the live experience, 'Show Me Your Hands' was an obvious choice to play on stage. Clarkin told *MetalTalk*'s album review show that it was inspired by a particularly enthusiastic German audience. The 3.48 radio edit included on the 2019 *Dance Of The Black Tattoo* compilation condenses the keyboard break, cuts out the guitar solo entirely and fades out the final minute early.

'Storm Baby' (6:13)

Lost On The Road To Eternity is the first album since *Brand New Morning* in 2004 not to include an unmistakable ballad. This song, with its beautiful piano and impassioned vocal in the verse, comes closest before it gives way in the chorus to a heavy guitar riff that's strangely reminiscent of Deep Purple's 'Smoke On The Water'. Although it's another tune that might have been cut by a minute or so without losing a great deal, it ultimately turns into a stomping, and extremely catchy, classic rock anthem. Clarkin delivers a solo that's simple yet effective over the top of the guitar riff.

'Welcome To The Cosmic Cabaret' (8:08)

While this isn't a particularly prog-sounding album in terms of musical complexity, it does include a couple of longer tracks that allow the band to stretch out and indulge their instrumental chops. 'Welcome To The Cosmic Cabaret' is only the third song in the catalogue to breach the eight-minute mark. For the most part, it's fairly conventional, if high-quality Magnum fare, with a low-key keyboard and percussion opening followed by a slow build to the chorus, augmented by shafts of crashing guitar chords. The pre-chorus and chorus are just sublime, turning the song on its head with inspired melodic lines. Special note should also go to Barrow's great sliding bass that traverses from the first chorus into the subsequent verse.

The song comes alive, however, in the instrumental section from 4.05, first with a thunderous Iron Maiden-esque guitar solo and a breakdown into jazzy keyboard motifs. Then, in the final minute and three-quarters, Clarkin indulges in some wonderful guitar improvisation against the backdrop of the atmospheric keyboard and percussion passage that opened the track.

The lyrics were inspired by the Turkish city of Istanbul. Clarkin also told GTFM Radio that the 'cosmic' in the title came from an old friend of his telling him: 'Hey man, you're really cosmic'.

'Lost On The Road To Eternity' (5:54)

Continuing another great opening run of songs, the title track is a breathtaking step into symphonic rock territory. The idea to include an orchestra on the track had its origins in the *Rock Meets Classic* European tour of 2017, organised by German metal vocalist Mat Sinner, in which Catley and Clarkin appeared and played five Magnum tracks accompanied by the Bohemian Symphony Orchestra. That encouraged Clarkin to employ German conductor Wolf Kerscheck to add orchestral parts to the tune, affording it a lavish and spectacular finish. The song also features an appearance by Tobias Sammet, vocalist with German heavy metal band Edguy and founder of supergroup Avantasia, to which Catley had contributed vocals since 2002. The resulting duet is incredibly effective, Catley's smooth voice combining with Sammet's grittier metal-style vocal.

Although it was an experiment that pushed the band beyond its comfort zone, 'Lost On The Road To Eternity' is a fantastic track, seamlessly amalgamating the traditional warm Magnum sound with a more adventurous power/symphonic metal flavour.

'Without Love' (5:55)

The lead track and promo single for the album, 'Without Love' is not typical of the record as a whole. It's constructed around an infectious drum and bass groove over which Clarkin lays down power chords. Catley's vocal, aided by Lee Small, a local singer-songwriter who had sung with Shy, Phenomena and Lionheart, is also a little different by Magnum standards, with short, snappy lines and plenty of repetition. The keyboards come in to bolster the chorus, but otherwise, this is all about rhythm and groove. The lyric video included a shortened version, while the acoustic treatment performed on *The Michael Ball Show* had more piano.

The lyrics were inspired by images of children in countries riven by conflict, such as Iraq and Syria, having to survive without parents. Clarkin was also influenced by pictures taken by his son-in-law while travelling in Vietnam, one of which was used for the cover of the single. As Clarkin told

GTFM Radio, the main thrust of the lyric was that while love 'couldn't cure everything... without love you don't have anything'.

'Tell Me What You Got To Say' (6:27)
Although it's not exactly an album of two halves, there's no doubt that the quality does dip slightly from this point on. 'Tell Me What You Got to Say' is a slow burner that takes time to work its charms. Barrow's pulsing bass line drives the song forward and Catley's singing is as heartfelt as ever. But it's the chorus, with its sweeping keyboard lines, that elevates the song beyond the mundane. Nonetheless, it's another tune that might have benefitted from a little editing; the guitar break at 4.12, for instance, is nice enough but lasts almost a minute.

'Ya Wanna Be Someone' (5:56)
This is another vibrant track characterised by elaborate keyboard flourishes and a catchy chorus riding on the top of a galloping rhythm section. Musically, there are echoes in the chorus of earlier tunes, particularly the verse of 'Like Brothers We Stand', although the tempo is very different and the backing vocals here take it in a slightly different direction. The experimental bridge at 3.54, with unaccompanied vocals improvising around the main theme that's then echoed by the guitar, is interesting but not entirely successful. The lyrics, which Clarkin told GTFM Radio were about a narcissistic individual with a 'huge ego problem', are pretty spiky. It has been widely assumed that the song is partly, at least, about Mark Stanway, with whom relations remained frosty.

'Forbidden Masquerade' (5:02)
Clarkin's cautionary tale of the dangers of drinking is an absorbing groove-based melodic rock track with a 1980s feel. Benton uses a range of keyboard sounds to provide the aural backdrop for the contrasting verse and chorus. There are a few clever vocal touches, from the choral-like texture of the bridge and outro to the half-hidden 'yeahs' in the final choruses.

'Glory To Ashes' (5:35)
The latest of Clarkin's anti-war hymns is not among his strongest. It has all the right ingredients, from the expressive repeating guitar motif to solemn piano interludes, topped off with a confident Catley vocal. Yet the tune is rather plain and forgettable and is ultimately Magnum at their most generic.

'King Of The World' (7:04)
While it's definitely the lesser of the album's two epics, there's just about enough going on here to hold the attention for seven minutes. The song is clearly meant to sound vast. It opens with a stately Eastern-style guitar and synth riff and then adopts a more bluesy vibe for the verse before ramping

the sombreness up again for the pre-chorus and chorus. For all this, it is rather plodding, even with the introduction of a chugging rhythm guitar in the second verse. The song certainly benefits from the change in tone at 4.40, where there's a breakdown into a beautiful but brief ambient piano and bass interlude and then a majestic drum and keyboard-driven section that then returns to the main theme.

Clarkin informed *MetalTalk* that the song focused on the founding figures of the world's religions and their influence over worshippers. Despite clear references to the story of Jesus – such as the 'scarlet robe' he was made to wear and 'just one kiss', referring to the kiss of Judas – the guitarist was keen to note that the message of the song was applicable to all religions.

The Serpent Rings (2020)

Personnel:
Tony Clarkin: guitar
Bob Catley: vocals
Rick Benton: keyboards
Dennis Ward: bass guitar
Lee Morris: drums
Additional Musicians:
Wolf Kerscheck Studio Orchestra: conducted by Wolf Kerscheck and arranged by Wolf Kerscheck on 'Where Are You Eden?' and by Rick Benton and Wolf Kerscheck on 'The Serpent Rings'
Rick Benton and Sheena Sear: orchestration on 'The Archway Of Tears' and 'Crimson On The White Sand'
Chris 'Beebe' Aldridge, Nick Dewhurst and Scott Ralph: brass on 'House Of Kings', arranged by Rick Benton
Liam Docherty, Lee Small, Jason Morgan and Brendon Riley: additional vocals on 'Where Are You Eden?', 'Madman Or Messiah', 'The Archway Of Tears', 'Not Forgiven', 'Man' and 'The Last One On Earth'
Produced at M2 Studios, Coven, by Tony Clarkin
Engineer: Sheena Sear
Release date: 17 January 2020 on SPV/Steamhammer
Cover Illustration: Rodney Matthews
Highest chart places: UK: 36, Germany: 5, Sweden: 29
Running time: 59:36

The Serpent Rings doesn't deviate too much from a formula which by now had become soundly tried and tested. There's a move back to a slightly heavier template and a little more experimentation with progressive structures, especially on the title track. However, the orchestral embellishments that were such a feature of *Lost On The Road To Eternity* were retained and, in places, even extended. Wolf Kersheck and his orchestra contributed to two tracks on the album and, elsewhere, a brass section was utilised for the first time since the acoustic *Keeping The Nite Light Burning* record in 1993.

There was one further line-up change when long-standing bassist Al Barrow announced his decision to leave the band in June 2019. Having moved with his family to Tennessee in the US, it was becoming more and more difficult for him to be away from home for a third of the year. As he told the *Roppongi Rocks* website in January 2022: 'it became an emotional battle each time in my head when I left to go to the UK'. He'd been with Magnum since 2001. Although he left the band, Barrow remained involved in designing artwork and merchandise and helping with social media. He was replaced by Dennis Ward, an American-born bassist and producer, formerly of German-based hard rock bands Pink Cream 69 and Unisonic.

Ward had produced Bob Catley's *Immortal* album in 2008 but joined Magnum following a recommendation from Tobias Sammet. His bass parts and backing vocals for the album were recorded at his own studio in Germany. Due to the subsequent COVID-19 pandemic, Ward was to record another Magnum album before his debut stage appearance with the band at the start of *The Monster Roars* tour in March 2022.

The album performed solidly across Europe, giving the group its highest position in Germany (number five) and also making number seven in Switzerland. The positions of 29 and 36 in Sweden and the UK respectively represented a slight decline from its predecessor. The 44-date European tour originally planned for March to May 2020 had to be rescheduled on a number of occasions due to the global pandemic, meaning that *The Serpent Rings* became the first Magnum album for many years not to have a designated tour of its own.

Matthews' cover is a classic sword and sorcery-style illustration. It depicts, in the artist's own words on his website blog, the storyteller figure as 'a reluctant warrior', kneeling as if to offer 'his sword and commitment'. Other interesting features include the symbols for the four elements ornamented on each pillar and a broken hourglass at the storyteller's feet, 'representing the ending of time and space and an acknowledgement of Eternity as the destiny of mankind'. The serpent rising above the storyteller, with its forked tongue, is meant to signify a lie, but there's some ambiguity in the use of blue and red on either side of the tongue, in the snake's eyes and via the shafts of light diffused through the windows, all of which, according to Matthews, can be taken to represent truth and lies respectively. Whatever the interpretation, it's a great cover and also a bit of a throwback to the classic sleeves of the early 1980s.

'Where Are You Eden?' (5:37)

This sumptuous opening track may be Magnum at their most bombastic, but it also manages to sound vital and modern. The opening is almost cinematic, with staccato strings not a million miles away from Alan Silvestri's famous theme for *The Avengers* movies. Thereafter, Benton's florid sweep of keyboards is central to the energy of a song that also makes full use of Wolf Kerscheck's orchestra, especially in the chorus and instrumental break. The choppy guitars and rumbling bass provide the backdrop for another great Catley vocal performance that rasps and soars at the right moments. A final highlight is the calming outro, combining romantic guitar and orchestral backing.

The one slight black mark against 'Where Are You Eden?' is the uncomfortable similarity of the riff to 'Live 'Til You Die' from *Escape From The Shadow Garden* (which itself, as noted earlier, borrows liberally from Saxon's '747 (Strangers In The Night)'. Given that Clarkin had written and recorded something in the region of 225 songs by the time of the release of this album, it's neither a surprise nor a criticism that certain themes and motifs were liable to repeat themselves. Furthermore, the wider musical context and production of the two songs are different enough to explain why it may not have concerned those close to the band.

'You Can't Run Faster Than Bullets' (5:40)
Following such a dramatic opening track, Clarkin's meditation on living in a war zone is a bit of a letdown. Built around a relatively uncomplicated heavy riff and blues structure, it's in line with the guitar-heavy approach of the material on *Sacred Blood 'Divine' Lies*. As always, there are a host of neat production touches, but in truth, it's not a song that lasts long in the memory.

'Madman Or Messiah' (5:18)
Speaking to Ray Shasho in January 2020, Catley identified the secret of the band's success: their ability to mix up their records with a range of varied material. A song like 'Madman Or Messiah' also indicates Clarkin's fondness for mixing things up within tracks, incorporating shifts in dynamics and mood as the rule rather than an exception. There's a bouncy, riff-based verse, a brief breakdown in rhythm for a pre-chorus with high-pitched vocals and then a typical Magnum-style melodic chorus, amplified by harmony vocals and Morris' liberal use of cymbals. The lingering deep synth chords in the bridge from 2.32 add an extra dimension, while Catley's Bruce Dickinson-style 'wo-oh' chant brings the song to a dramatic close.

A track dealing with what Clarkin himself described as 'self-proclaimed saviours' at the head of pseudo religions and cults, such as David Koresh at Waco in 1993 and Charles Manson during the 1960s, 'Madman Or Messiah' was one of the songs chosen for a radio edit. The version included on *The Dance Of The Black Tattoo* compilation omits the synth break and the chanted finish.

'The Archway Of Tears' (6:21)
This is the most accomplished song on the album and among the very best tunes of the reunion years. It fits a fairly classic Magnum template (developed on songs such as 'On A Storyteller's Night') of a haunting guitar and keyboard opening and verse that then builds rapidly through a brief pre-chorus to an all-out melodic rock chorus. When this works well, as it does here, it's mainly a result of the richness of the melody, the power of the arrangement and the passion in the vocal. Like 'Storyteller's Night', it also boasts one of Clarkin's most infectious guitar breaks from 3.53-4.26. There's also a clever chanted reprise of the chorus that is perfect for live audience participation.

While there are no clear indications about what the song means, it may well be referring to the entrance of the former Birmingham Union Workhouse in Victorian times. It was the place where those experiencing severe poverty were assessed for possible entry into the workhouse, where they would be expected to undertake hard labour in return for food and shelter. As the Birmingham Conservation Trust website puts it: 'Its evocative name reflects the sorrow suffered by new arrivals as families were split by gender and age to relevant living and working areas'. The building was in the local news around the time the album was being written, as there had been a campaign to preserve it. This was eventually lost when it was demolished in 2017. The lyrics, depicting the lack of hope and endless toil of those who 'work a lifetime', are a close fit.

This was one of only two songs from the album (the other was 'Where Are You Eden?') played on stage when Magnum returned to live performance in 2022.

'Not Forgiven' (5:48)

A full-blooded rock track, this plays a similar role on this album as 'Without Love' did on its predecessor. It's propelled by a bright AC/DC-like guitar riff and a rhythm track that's about as funky as Magnum are likely to get at this stage in their career, with new boys Morris and Ward combining to great effect. As elsewhere across the album, there are some lovely piano licks and fills and at 3.48, there's a nice moment where the descending piano pattern is mirrored by repetition of the word 'forgiven' with a number of voices in a round format. The promo single from the album, it's likely 'Not Forgiven' would have been played live on the accompanying tour had it gone ahead. The song is based on the Italian theatrical character of the harlequin (which is alluded to in the lyric video and the cover art) and the idea that people can use masks to hide their true intentions and feelings.

'The Serpent Rings' (6:47)

This is one of the few latter-day tracks in which the band indulge their prog leanings. According to Clarkin, it was a song that started out as a 'science fiction story' and ended up 'as an eerie and somewhat creepy fairy tale'. References to 'dragon clouds' and 'flaming horses... on silent wings' place this firmly in fantasy territory. Yet, as the guitarist told Bruce Mee in *Fireworks* magazine, he based some of the lyrics on real places close to where he lived. For instance, 'mercia green' relates to the Forest of Mercia close to Cannock in Staffordshire while the 'iron horse' that 'rises into Azure', as well as alluding to the old-fashioned term for steam locomotives, probably relates to the horse sculptures that can be viewed along the Wolverhampton to Birmingham railway line. The music is grandiose, atmospheric and intricate at turns, as one would expect. The moment when the tune suddenly leaps up to the 'serpent rings on every finger gold and silver' refrain, with every syllable accentuated, is unexpected and deeply satisfying. Beyond this, the best section is the extended instrumental passage from 4.12-6.28 that moves from bluesy guitar to dreamy synth and spooky strings and, finally, an expressive Clarkin guitar solo.

135

'House Of Kings' (4:46)

A strange amalgam of hard rock and soft jazz, at its core, this is a pretty heavy tune that Catley delivers with an almost metal sensibility. But it's lightened by the brass ensemble and a range of delicate keyboard and piano touches. The piano break after the second chorus is almost easy listening, lounge music. It shouldn't work and, on this occasion, it doesn't.

'The Great Unknown' (5:27)

Despite an opening that sounds like a 1980s power ballad, this builds into a richly anthemic track of real substance. Catley's voice is full of anguish and emotion as he navigates a series of gorgeous melodies. However, it's not the only song towards the end of the record that might have benefitted from a little instrumental variation or some judicious editing.

'Man' (5:31)

This is a fairly heavy-handed treatise on the impact that man's 'greed and insatiability' have had on the environment. As Clarkin noted in the album's press release: 'We destroy nature just to make an even bigger profit and we are seeing the negative results of that attitude more clearly now than ever before'. There are plenty of interesting musical ideas here, from the opening filmic keyboard swells and pulsing synth touches to the slight hint of a reggae rhythm and then the unusual percussive triangle ending. Yet, as is often the case with Magnum, it's the strength of the melodies that see the song through.

'The Last One On Earth' (3:32)

This is a simple, understated track dominated by an elegant piano motif and another exuberant vocal performance. Like a fair many of the songs towards the end of later Magnum albums, there's more depth than is first apparent, particularly in its mellow soundscapes and the unusual two-part middle eight from 1.57-2.40.

'Crimson On The White Sand' (4:53)

Not dissimilar in tone to 'The Great Unknown' and 'The Last One On Earth', this romantic piece ensures that the album ends in a stately fashion. Based on a sumptuous piano theme, it builds into a mid-paced melodic rock behemoth with yearning guitar and dense multi-tracked vocal harmonies. Like much of the second half of the album, it's fascinating to listen to and expertly put together, but should perhaps be filed under solid rather than classic Magnum fare.

The Monster Roars (2022)

Personnel:
Tony Clarkin: guitars
Bob Catley: vocals
Rick Benton: keyboards
Dennis Ward: bass and backing vocals
Lee Morris: drums
Additional Musicians:
Chris 'Beebe' Aldridge and Nick Dewhurst: brass on 'No Steppin' Stones'
Shaz Benton: additional vocals on 'The Present And The Past', 'No Steppin' Stones' and 'The Day After The Night Before'
Produced at M2 Studios, Coven, UK by Tony Clarkin
Engineer: Sheena Sear
Release date: 14 January 2022 on SPV/Steamhammer
Cover Photo: 'The Monster' played by Martin Brennan, created by Kelly Odell and photographed by Rob Barrow; rear cover photograph, Andrew Farrier
Highest chart places: UK: 51, Germany: 5, Sweden: 29
Running time: 58:27

As with many bands, COVID-19 scuppered touring plans and pushed Magnum into an enforced hibernation. But the postponement and eventual cancellation of *The Serpent Rings* tour did mean that Clarkin was able to start work on new material even earlier in the cycle. A whole album had been written and partly recorded by the autumn of 2020, meaning that, as Catley told the *Gorey Guardian* in November 2020, 'we're a year up front with the recording of the new album'. But the band took six months off to accommodate their engineer Sheena Sear's pregnancy, returning in the summer of 2021 to finish the record.

This was the first album since 2004 not to feature a Rodney Matthews illustration. Matthews was busy with other projects and so the band looked at alternatives to depict the 'monster' of the title. In the end, they chose a photograph of Clarkin's son-in-law heavily made up as a horned monster. The idea had been to recreate an image Clarkin had found on make-up artist Kelly Odell's website. Only later did the guitarist discover that the monster was based on the mythical figure of Krampus, popular in the folklore of central and eastern Europe. Luckily, however, the story around Krampus, who is supposed to scare children who misbehave at Christmastime, fitted the lyrics of the title track.

The Monster Roars is another solid album. It has fewer high points, perhaps, than its predecessor but is a little more consistent. Not surprisingly, there's no radical reinvention of the Magnum sound, but there are enough great tunes and inventive touches to ensure that the fanbase and critics alike remained satisfied. Most important was the return of the band to the live arena. Like the recording of the album, *The Monster Roars* tour was split into two halves.

The first part, from March to May 2022, took in 30 dates in eight European countries (including a number of support slots in Germany with Swiss rockers Gotthard), while the second leg in September covered the remaining UK dates. Three dates rescheduled due to COVID-19 for early December were topped off with the 50th-anniversary show in Wolverhampton on 10 December.

'The Monster Roars' (3:57)
The album opens with the title track and one of its most musically dynamic songs. Clarkin's tale of the things children imagine and fear that keep them awake at night is similar in theme to 'Dragons Are Real' and also brings to mind the live version of 'On A Storyteller's Night'. Yet, musically, it's quite different from both. It alternates between a fabulously harmonised wistful verse and a thunderously heavy and raw chorus, while the intense, fluctuating instrumental section from 2.14 suggests that it could have been extended into an archetypal Magnum epic.

'Remember' (5:06)
Another of Clarkin's nostalgic ruminations on the past, this one centres on the band's early days playing chart hits at the Rum Runner during the 1970s. The DJ mentioned in the bridge 'playing records that no one had heard' is none other than Catley, who was employed to spin discs between the live sets. It's a lovely tune, enhanced by some subtle contributions from Ward and Morris and a number of great licks, as well as a surprising classically-infused coda courtesy of Benton. 'Remember' would surely have been played live on the accompanying tour had space been made for more than two cuts from the album.

'All You Believe In' (5:01)
One of the album's busy, upbeat songs, 'All You Believe In' demonstrates the key role Benton had established in the band. Guitar and keyboard motifs interweave, repeat and echo one another ingeniously. Benton's piano takes the lead role for much of the track, including the breakdown that follows the magnificent bridge and comes before a harmonious Brian May-inspired guitar solo.

'I Won't Let You Down' (3:57)
The first promo single from the album, this is a nice, if fairly light, tune built on an unusual stuttering riff. The lyrics are a standard Clarkin declaration of care for those who 'stumble', although the guitarist told *TotalRock*'s 'From the Inside' podcast that he was imagining, specifically, the support provided by the partner of someone who had suffered a nervous breakdown.

'The Present Not The Past' (5:27)
One of the album's more inventive tunes, this moves between slow, melancholic verses, hard rock power chords and a characteristically layered

melodic refrain in the chorus. A call for people to live in the moment, the second verse references a meeting Clarkin had with a homeless man during the late 1960s. He gave the guitarist a number of predictions for the future in exchange for a cup of tea (changed to 'one glass of water' in the song).

'No Steppin' Stones' (3:57)
The second promo single, with its prominent horn accompaniment, seems, on the surface, to be a move away from the traditional Magnum sound. But it's not as if the band haven't been here before. And it's an uplifting track full of energy and ideas, from the concert chatter at the beginning to the lovely interlude at 2.33 with synth vocal effects and a gorgeous melodic bass line. It's another song that would have sounded great live.

'That Freedom Word' (4:52)
A serious discourse on the nature of freedom and what it means in different contexts, this is another song that moves seamlessly from slow and soft to fast and heavy. The three main sections suggest a slight progressive influence. We move from a lilting guitar lullaby based on a bedrock of keyboard chords to the fabulously hooky Maiden-esque chorus; after two runs through, there's a change of time signature and mood to the euphonic bridge. 'That Freedom Word' is excellently constructed and one of the album's most satisfying songs.

'Your Blood Is Violence' (6:44)
The longest track on the album also has the most convoluted origins. Originally about the four horsemen of the apocalypse, Clarkin ditched it all except the riff and wrote a new song around that. The whole band are on fine form here, with special mention going to the undulating bass lines of Ward. It's possibly Catley's most versatile performance on the record, with a full-throated soaring vocal in the chorus and a more restrained performance in the verse and bridge. In the 'You've got money in your pocket' section, he even does a reasonable impression of Jethro Tull's Ian Anderson.

'Walk The Silent Hours' (4:51)
Inspired by a documentary Clarkin watched about the White Helmets, a volunteer medical organisation operating during the Syrian Civil War, this is a deep contemplative ballad. It includes some gorgeous contributions from Benton but doesn't go anywhere that you wouldn't expect. It's a pity space couldn't be found for a guitar or piano solo.

'The Day After The Night Before' (4:23)
This is an upbeat, rollicking tune documenting the fictitious overthrow of one political regime by another. It's one of those songs that is hard to listen to without a smile on your face. The main riff, underpinned by a massive rhythm track, is fairly routine, but as is common with Magnum, it's lifted by the

quality of the melody. There's also an inspired progressive-style synth break just before the middle eight. 'The Day After The Night Before' was the second track from the album played live during the 2022 tour.

'Come Holy Men' (5:01)

11 tracks in and the standard has barely dipped. 'Come Holy Men' is rocky and majestic in a way only Magnum can successfully pull off. It's built on a hooky but fragile-sounding guitar riff and throbbing bass that explodes into a heavy pre-chorus, with Catley straining in true metal style. The release comes with a fabulously evocative chorus that's as good as anything on the album. Clarkin finally lets rip with an all-too-brief solo in the last minute of the track.

'Can't Buy Yourself A Heaven' (5:00)

Clarkin told *TotalRock* that the final track was one that he struggled to get right. Originally written on an acoustic guitar, the song itself is fairly straightforward but the centrepiece is the lengthy guitar solo from 3.00-4.02 that Clarkin notes was rewritten and re-recorded a number of times and edited down. Supported by lush keyboard soundscapes, it sounds great but seems almost to exist separately from what is otherwise the weakest track on the album.

Here Comes The Rain (2024)

Personnel:
Tony Clarkin: guitars
Bob Catley: vocals
Rick Benton: keyboards
Dennis Ward: bass and backing vocals
Lee Morris: drums
Additional Musicians:
Chris 'Beebe' Aldridge and Nick Dewhurst: brass on 'Some Kind Of Treachery' and 'The Seventh Darkness' [NOTE: Aldridge plays saxophone – a woodwind instrument – on 'The Seventh Darkness', but this is credited as 'brass']
Liam Doherty, Brendon Riley and Kyle Lamley: additional vocals on 'Run Through The Shadows', 'The Seventh Darkness' and 'I Wanna Live'
Rick Benton and Sheena Sear: All string arrangements
Produced at M2 Studios, Coven, by Tony Clarkin
Engineer: Sheena Sear
Release date: 12 January 2024
Cover Illustration: Rodney Matthews
Highest chart places: UK: 68, Germany: 2, Sweden: 23
Running time: 50:09

Work on Magnum's 23rd studio album began much like most of the previous half dozen or so. Clarkin worked up and demoed a number of songs that were then filtered down and played to Catley, with the rest of the band joining in the recording at a later date. Once again based at M2 Studios, vocals and guitars were put down through the early months of 2023, with drums, keyboards and bass added later. Speaking in January 2024, Lee Morris noted that, unusually for many bands, Magnum recorded the drums towards the end of the sessions as the arrangements and tempo often changed through the process. A studio update from June 2023 noted that the drums were 'done and dusted', with keyboards and bass added over the summer. 'Everyone played their part without me dictating anything', Clarkin noted in the album's press release, 'everyone just instinctively played what their inspiration told them'.

The sound of the album tapped into various elements of the band's past. More overtly melodic and keyboard-infused than the previous few albums, the compositions and melody lines were also slightly more straightforward. The step back from more heavy instrumentation and the relatively moderate pace of a number of the tracks was especially reminiscent of *Princess Alice And The Broken Arrow*. In one or two places, Clarkin did steer away from conventional arrangements and instrumentation. The use of brass, augmented by saxophone, continued on 'The Seventh Darkness'. More significantly, the band broke new ground with one song, 'Broken City', comprising just vocals, keyboards and strings.

Ultimately, *Here Comes The Rain* benefits from the consistent quality of the songwriting. Coming in at a concise 50 minutes, it is the shortest Magnum album since the 1990s and all the better for it. There's precious little fat on the bones of these songs and a directness and economy in the delivery that isn't always apparent in the post-reunion albums. More than all this, however, *Here Comes The Rain* is the best collection of Clarkin tunes since *On The Thirteenth Day* and stands as one of the strongest entries in the 21st-century Magnum catalogue.

Rodney Matthews was available again to provide the striking cover art. The original idea, based on the title *Some Kind Of Treachery*, involved ravens and vultures swooping down among war-damaged buildings in 'an Eastern-styled' cityscape. This was jettisoned when the album title was altered and replaced by the storyteller holding up an umbrella against an incoming 'armada of mechanical ravens and vultures with malevolent red eyes'. Clarkin also asked for the inclusion of the schoolboy with the catapult (from the *Moonking*, *Sacred Blood* and *Lost On The Road To Eternity* covers) and his dog, whom Matthews based on his own border collie. The back cover/left-hand side of the painting includes a space-age telecommunications tower in the background. The colour palette of an orange moon against a periwinkle blue sky was inspired by an evening walk Matthews took just a few hours after the first discussion of the *Here Comes The Rain* concept with Clarkin.

The release of *Here Comes The Rain* came alongside the most tragic of news. On 7 January 2024, less than a week before the album's release date, Tony Clarkin died. His family announced that his death came after a short illness. There had been some indication that the guitarist was not in the best of health when it was revealed, just before Christmas 2023, that he had a rare spinal condition that would not allow him to undertake the planned UK and European tour dates the following year. Yet, the news came as a shock to friends and fans of the band, leading to an outpouring of love and respect for this most singular of musicians and songwriters.

'Run Into The Shadows' (5:22)

This punchy tune continues the late career consistency of Magnum's opening album tracks. Introduced by an alluring AOR-ish keyboard refrain, swiftly undergirded by drums, bass and guitars, this is high-quality melodic rock from start to finish. The melody line in the verse is simple, echoing the main riff, with variations emerging in the pre-chorus. Catley's vocals are sublime, moving from a low register in the verse to the precisely harmonised falsetto chorus. It also includes a typically high-quality middle eight. The repeated sections towards the close of the song include some fine additional vocals from the backing singers and Catley. While it might have been enhanced by a guitar solo, this is a great way to kick things off. With its lyrical focus on conflict and warzones, 'Run Into The Shadows' establishes a thematic template for a great deal of what follows.

'Here Comes The Rain' (4:36)

Despite a decrease in tempo, the title track maintains the quality and sturdy constitution of the opening tune. Built on a winding, sinewy guitar riff, 'Here Comes The Rain' boasts a light, almost ethereal vocal line that then morphs into a dark, anthemic chorus. In many respects, it's a typical mid-paced Clarkin composition, yet one that manages to sound fresh and vital. Special mention should go to Ward's animated bassline that bounces around to great effect underneath the layers of keyboards, guitar and vocals in the song's final minute and a half. Described by Catley as a song about 'coming under fire in a warzone', the lyrics offer little hope and contain more than a hint of resignation. 'There's no silver bullet', Catley sings in the middle eight, 'Made in this world/That will bring us together'.

'Some Kind Of Treachery' (4:31)

The first of a series of ballads on the album, 'Some Kind Of Treachery' is a solid composition located in a luxurious soundscape. It begins with a beautiful piano refrain, echoing classic 1980s Asia, augmented by Catley's soulful, yearning vocal. The chorus ups the tempo, delivering a simple but pleasingly effective melody. With plenty of keyboard and orchestral flourishes, Benton is the star of this one, undertaking most of the instrumental heavy lifting, while Clarkin's guitar sits comfortably buried in the mix. There's nothing to surprise the listener here, but it's delightfully constructed and performed.

'After The Silence' (4:35)

If one song on *Here Comes The Rain* could be described as an archetype of the classic Magnum sound, this is it. One of a number of tracks with an atmospheric synth opening, it soon jumps into action with a satisfying combination of keyboard swirls and chugging rhythmic guitar. The chorus, in particular, with its channelling of the melodic rock of the *Wings Of Heaven* and *Princess Alice* eras, is pure bliss. The one let-down, consistent across much of the album, is the absence of a guitar or keyboard solo that might have added some variety to the last minute and a half of the song.

'Blue Tango' (5:26)

The first 'single', 'Blue Tango' was released on social media in November 2023. Described by the band as 'a riff-rock number that makes you want to move your feet', it has a similar 'feel good' vibe as 1990's 'Rockin' Chair', which had been a crowd favourite on *The Monster Roars* tour. The opening, incorporating the sound of a coin-operated jukebox, sets the tune firmly in the same nostalgic territory as the previous album's 'Remember'. It's certainly good fun. The guitar line, straight out of the ZZ Top playbook, is catchy and there's a lively organ solo from Benton. Ultimately, however, it doesn't quite have the same depth as the rest of the album and is probably the weakest track.

'The Day He Lied' (4:34)

The album's sixth track is a stirring, melancholic ballad cast in a similar mould as 2012's 'Putting Things In Place'. Keyboards and synths again dominate the sonic architecture, but there are some fine percussive touches from Morris, especially in the transition to the chorus and the marching drum pattern that brings the song to a close. It should also be noted that it's Clarkin's aching guitar line that introduces the song and bolsters the melody in the chorus. Once again, however, it's a little surprising that Clarkin didn't include an extended keyboard or guitar break.

'The Seventh Darkness' (4:43)

Released at the very beginning of 2024 as the second pre-album promo track, this is a catchy song infused with a number of inventive production ideas. The main riff, featuring brass layered on top of Clarkin's guitar, drives the song forward, and despite not having a conventional chorus, it doesn't lag for a second. There's a lovely guitar break after the first verse, a seamless slowing of tempo into the middle eight and some clever vocal embellishments in the third verse. However, the undoubted centrepiece of the track is the duelling saxophone and guitar interlude between 2.18 and 2.45, which sounds wonderfully unhinged. A song about 'dirty, rotten politicians' – one of Clarkin's favourite lyrical themes – this is a sparkling tune, sequenced perfectly between two of the album's more sombre numbers.

'Broken City' (4:39)

The album's final ballad is also its least conventional: Catley's voice is accompanied only by Benton's keyboards. It consists of two repeated sections: a stripped-down verse with simple backing and a more elaborate chorus featuring piano arpeggios and harp. There's a slightly more upbeat middle eight, but overall, it's an effectively poignant track topped by a reliably emotive Catley vocal. The last of the triumvirate of songs (after 'Run Into The Shadows' and 'Here Comes The Rain') that deal with contemporary trouble spots and warzones, the lyrics are purposefully vague, although it may be that the title refers to Ukrainian cities, such as Mariupol and Popasna, decimated in 2022 as a result of the Russian offensive.

'I Wanna Live' (5:28)

Here Comes The Rain defiantly avoids the tendency of the previous few Magnum records to lose momentum and peter out towards the end. Indeed, its final two songs are possibly the best on the album. 'I Wanna Live' is a punchy, melodious juggernaut of a track. There's a carefully posed equilibrium here between the warm sheet of keyboards and rippling piano on one hand and the crunch of the guitars on the other. Ward's bass line, meanwhile, offers both robust support and melodic intervention, weaving in and out of the transitions between sections, while Clarkin delivers a soaring

David Gilmour/Steve Rothery-inspired solo. The song takes a left turn in the last minute and a half with a wonderful organ-based coda, complete with atmospheric keyboards and vocal effects. One of the highlights of the album, this is a song that would easily have slotted onto one of the band's more commercial mid-to-late 1980s records.

'Borderline' (6:15)

The album closes with another example of Clarkin's ability to create muscular, melodic hard rock of the highest quality. Opening with vaguely Middle Eastern-sounding vocal effects, the composition quickly shifts into conventional full-band mode. There's no time to settle, however, as Clarkin's surging guitar break at 1.07 ushers in the core of the track with its stomping, almost funky, rhythmic urgency. The melody, in common with much of the album, is simple but infectious and Catley delivers it with his customary confidence. Clarkin's instrumental contributions, meanwhile, are a high point of the album. In a record short on guitar breaks, he provides three here; on the third, between 3.26 and 3.52, he really lets loose for the first and only time on the album. The rhythm section of Morris and Ward is also on top form. At 4.54, there's a short transition that flows into a lovely piano interlude (reminiscent of the Alan Parsons Project). It's short-lived and the song fades out, leaving us with a mini 'Don't Wake The Lion'-style epic that is great but might have been even better had it been extended with one further section.

Hard Rain, 1996-2000

After the 1995 split, Tony Clarkin and Bob Catley reconvened to work together on material as Hard Rain. The name was taken from a lyric in one of the band's early songs, 'You'd Start a Fight (In An Empty House)': 'Hard rain love to see it fallin'/Wash you, get you out of my blood'. Catley recalled his experience of working with Clarkin in Hard Rain in a 2012 interview with Rok Podgrajšek:

> Hard Rain was a relief. 'Sod this, let's just be a rock 'n' roll band again'. And it was great. I really enjoyed working with Tony on this. We used some of the songs that might have been on the next Magnum album but became the first Hard Rain album. So the first Hard Rain album was a cross between Magnum and Hard Rain, while the second was a total rock 'n' roll album, which had nothing to do with Magnum.

Rainer Hänsel, who had promoted Magnum's final tour in continental Europe, signed Hard Rain for CBH Records in Germany. The self-titled debut came out in March 1997 but was only available on import in the UK and made little impression there, in Germany or elsewhere in Europe. The second record, *When The Good Times Come*, released by Eagle Records in May 1999, was no more successful. The reviews were less complimentary and the band did some short tours, but the audiences weren't substantial.

Clarkin now tends to recall Hard Rain as an experiment that failed. He dismissed the band in a 2017 interview with *eonmusic* as 'a crazy idea' and told *HRH Rock Mag* that it 'flopped badly'. In the same interview, Catley described the Hard Rain days as 'a lot of fun' while Al Barrow has commented that things weren't taken as seriously within the band as in the reformed Magnum. The thanks in the liner notes of the debut album to 'the landlord and staff of the Black Swan' indicates where the focus often was.

In the meantime, Catley had joined forces with songwriter Gary Hughes of melodic rock band Ten and, in November 1998, produced an excellent solo album, *The Tower*. Hughes had been given the directive to 'write the album that Magnum could have made between *Storyteller*'s and *Wings Of Heaven* if I was in the band'. Catley was keen to pursue this direction and so, with his second solo album *Legends* about to be released, he left Hard Rain in September 1999. Hard Rain, meanwhile, lay in abeyance while Clarkin decided what to do next.

Hard Rain (1997)

The debut album from Hard Rain was recorded between February and December 1996 at Mark Stuart's Mad Hat Studios, then situated in Walsall. Tony Clarkin produced and it was engineered and mixed by Mike Cowling, who had worked on the previous three Magnum albums. Clarkin seems to have handled all the instrumentation with Catley on vocals, supported by backing vocalists Jackie Dean and Wendy Peddie.

Catley and Clarkin were always anxious to remind people that Hard Rain was not Magnum. The guitarist assured the music correspondent of the *Birmingham Evening Mail* that Hard Rain were more than simply Magnum Mark II:

There are things on the album that Magnum would have done – but there are other things there that they wouldn't. For example, we've got two female backing singers who, incidentally, sound sensational.

But given that many of the tracks here had been written for a planned Magnum album, it's reasonable to judge it on those terms. One of the problems for Clarkin was that in trying to step away from what he considered to be the Magnum template, he moved into fairly generic rock territory. Stripped of his former band's trademark sound and idiosyncrasies, the music is, in truth, a little bland. What is more, it's difficult to deny that, regardless of style, *Hard Rain* was the weakest collection of songs Clarkin had written. If it had come out as a Magnum album, it would have found itself at the bottom of the pile, and by some distance.

That isn't to say there's not some decent material here. 'I Must Have Been Blind' is a good country-style ballad, while 'Perpetual Commotion' is the best of the hard rock tunes. 'Stop Me From Lovin' You', released as a single in Germany, is another engaging ballad, though it sounds uncomfortably similar to late-period ELO. The best song on the album is 'Different Kind Of Love', a lengthy pop-rock track with a number of sections of almost Magnum-style epic proportions.

The album was re-released in 1999 by Receiver Records as *Perpetual Commotion*.

When The Good Times Come (1999)

The band that Clarkin and Catley put together to tour the first album also recorded the follow-up to *Hard Rain*. The Barrow brothers, Al and Rob, joined on bass and drums respectively; Paul Hodson, who had worked with John Parr and Dante Fox, among others, was the new keyboard player and Sue McCloskey became second vocalist, although she only takes the lead on one song on the album. The record also features contributions from the 'Boss Horns' and harmonica from Brian Bannister. As with the debut, it was recorded at Mad Hat in Walsall, produced by Clarkin and engineered by Mike Cowling.

More than the debut, this strikes out in a range of stylistic directions. While hard rock remains at the core of the sound, there are experiments with jazz ('Showtime') and even funk ('Eat It Up'). The album certainly sounds less like Magnum than the debut, but there's plenty to enjoy here. 'Rock Me In Ya Cradle' is a punchy hard rock tune, 'No One Can Show You The Way' works well as a refined FM radio-style ballad, while 'Never Say Never' has a chorus as vast as some of Clarkin's 1980s compositions.

Epilogue

Tributes to Tony Clarkin flooded in within hours of his death. Contemporaries such as Fish, once of Marillion, noted Clarkin's qualities as a man, a musician and a songwriter, while Tobias Sammet recalled the profound influence of Clarkin's music on him: 'Without Magnum, there would be no Edguy or Avantasia, you always have been a huge inspiration'. Challenging the common dismissal of the band as 'also rans' in the 1980s rock and metal scene, journalists such as Mick Wall and Dave Ling recalled the quality of the Magnum's discography and live performances. 'Deeply melodious and rich in depth and colour', Ling remarked in his *Classic Rock* tribute, 'a Clarkin composition was always instantly recognisable'.

Magnum never repeated the mainstream success of the 1980s, and neither were they ever likely to give in to the transformation of the music industry and the relative marginalisation of guitar rock within 21st-century music culture. Yet, frequent releases allowed them to stay current and relevant, eschewing the 'legacy rock' label that Clarkin despised. It also meant they could perform in front of thousands of fans in the UK and continental Europe, whose devotion to the band had, if anything, tightened in the age of online fan groups and social media. In view of all this, Ling's assessment that Clarkin's 'body of work' was 'comparable with the best of best' is far from an exaggeration.

It's unlikely Magnum will continue without Clarkin. Not only was he the sole songwriter, but he was also undisputedly the band's leader, the 'engine room' of Magnum, as one tribute put it. If the band dies with him, we're nonetheless left with one of the most consistent, varied and richly textured bodies of work in British rock music.

Live Albums

The list of live albums here includes official releases only. They have been arranged in order of recording rather than release.

Days Of Wonder (2000; Recorded 1976)

This is a special recording of Magnum playing a live set before the release of the debut album. It is taken from a performance at the Railway Inn in Birmingham, where the band had a regular slot every Thursday during 1976, although we don't know the exact date of the recording. The album came about when one of Clarkin's friends found the recording, which had been made with a microphone and a Revox machine, in his loft. Clarkin mentions in the liner notes that at first, 'it sounded like it had been recorded through a sock', but the sound quality improved after being EQ'd. In total, the album includes six songs that were included on the 1978 debut album (including a version of 'Kingdom Of Madness' that Clarkin thinks may have been learnt by the band the day before), a raft of earlier songs, including the four outtakes which were originally intended for the debut and even two tracks that ended up on 1979's *Magnum II*. There's also an early version of Dion's doo-wop hit 'Runaround Sue'.

Marauder (1980)

The album that changed the band's fortunes, *Marauder* still sounds great today. Recorded at the famous Marquee club in London in December 1979 by Leo Lyons, who had produced *Magnum II*, it was then mixed by Chris Tsangarides at the Marquee's own studio. Tsangarides was to later make his name as a formidable hard rock and heavy metal producer, well known for his work with Thin Lizzy, Judas Priest, Bruce Dickinson and many others. Jet Records decided which songs would be on the album and which would be left over for the 'Magnum Live' EP, although all 12 tracks were included on the two-disc Castle reissue in 2005. Catley's observation in the liner notes that *Marauder* 'had the power that was sometimes missing in the studio' hits the nail on the head.

Invasion Live (1989; Recorded 1982)

In 1989, Receiver Records released this nine-track recording of Magnum's set supporting label mate Ozzy Osbourne on the *Diary Of A Madman* tour in 1982. The performance is taken from the 29 April show at Nashville's Municipal Auditorium. Clarkin recalls in the *Marauder* expanded edition sleeve notes that the recording equipment had been brought along for Ozzy but was used for Magnum 'to make sure it all worked'. The setlist is pretty evenly split between the band's three albums at the time, with 'Runaround Sue' as the finale. The versions of 'Soldier Of The Line' and 'Sacred Hour', two of the best recordings here, had already been released as the live record of the four-track 'Live In America' EP in late 1982.

The River Sessions (2004; Recorded 1985)

This is another fascinating live recording from the 1980s that didn't get a conventional release until much later. Recorded at Glasgow's Mayfair (now the Garage) on 28 May 1985, it was originally broadcast on Radio Clyde. It was released in 2004 by River Records, a company specialising in 'in concert' broadcasts from Scottish radio stations. The tracklist is dominated by material from the then-new *On A Storyteller's Night* LP (no fewer than eight tracks), with a smattering of *Chase The Dragon* tunes and one each from *Kingdom Of Madness*, *Magnum II* and *The Eleventh Hour*. It's one of Magnum's best live recordings, summing up the confident performance of a band whose fortunes had just turned for the better. Highlights include storming versions of 'The Prize', 'How Far Jerusalem' and 'Sacred Hour'.

The Spirit (1991)

Magnum's last album for Polydor, *The Spirit* is a great souvenir of a period when the band were still playing arenas in the UK. There had been plans to release a live album for some time but recordings of individual songs were used instead for single B-sides. During the short 'The Spirit' tour in November and December 1990, however, a number of shows were recorded specifically for a live release. (This tour shouldn't be confused with the *The Spirit* UK and European tour arranged in September and October 1991 to promote this album). Originally intended as a double album, it was cut to a single to save money. The final selection is something of a greatest hits package, with material evenly distributed between the recent release and the main 1980s albums – three apiece from *Goodnight LA*, *Storyteller's Night* and *Vigilante* and two each from *Wings Of Heaven* and *Chase The Dragon* – as well as the evergreen 'Kingdom Of Madness'. One of Magnum's strongest live collections, *The Spirit* includes great renditions of 'Les Morts Dansant', 'On A Storyteller's Night' and 'When The World Comes Down' among others.

The Last Dance (1996)

The band's first live double album was originally also marketed as 'the last ever recordings from Magnum'. Recorded during the band's farewell tour in Cologne on 24 November 1995, it was distributed by the German label SPV and came out in mainland Europe in May 1996. The tracklist includes 18 songs from each of the band's 11 studio albums with the exception of 1983's *The Eleventh Hour* and 1992's *Sleepwalking*, and incorporated a tremendous, elongated version of 'Kingdom Of Madness' followed by a Barker drum solo. All told it's a joyous listening experience and one of Magnum's most complete live recordings.

Stronghold (1997)

This is the UK version of *The Last Dance*, released in 1997 by Receiver Records. It includes two extra tracks at the end of each side from the 1992

Christmas concerts and boasts a Rodney Matthew fantasy sleeve of a fortress on an isolated hill, presumably to reflect the new title.

Wings Of Heaven Live (2008)
Magnum's second double live album is a record of the 2007-08 *Wings Of Heaven* anniversary tour. The first record mixes classics and three tracks from the most recent *Princess Alice* album. The second features a complete rendition of the *Wings Of Heaven* album in sequence. It's great to hear these songs again, albeit with a heavier sheen reflecting where the band were sonically at the time. The recordings were taken from French and UK dates between 2-18 November 2007.

Escape From The Shadow Garden: Live 2014 (2015)
There's a slightly rawer, unvarnished feel to this single disc/record. The crowd noise is prominent, making the listener feel a part of the experience. The tracklist also gives due attention to the recent material, with the first six songs all drawn from the three previous albums. It's probably Magnum's heaviest live album, with the one-two punch of 'Live 'Til You Die' and 'Black Skies' especially impressive and the most dynamic rendition of 'How Far Jerusalem' for some years.

Live At The Symphony Hall (2019)
Magnum's third double live album is a homecoming gig, recorded on 19 April 2018 at Birmingham's Symphony Hall. There are some lovely moments here, such as Tobias Sammet reprising his guest vocal slot on 'Lost On The Road To Eternity' and a thunderous version of 'Don't Wake The Lion'. Catley's voice, not surprisingly, is harsher and less flexible than on previous recordings. By and large, this suits the heavier material in this set but even ballads like 'Your Dreams Won't Die' and 'When The World Comes Down' still hold up well.

Live at KK's Steel Mill (2024) – Double CD and DVD
Released as part of the *Here Comes The Rain* package (the DVD came with the studio CD and the live CD with the deluxe box set), this is a solid representation of the band's December 2022 anniversary gig. The setlist is identical to most of the *The Monster Roars* tour, with material drawn from every stage of Magnum's career. A rejuvenated 'Days Of No Trust', 'Wild Swan', 'The Flood' and 'On A Storyteller's Night' stand out as particularly memorable. The concert (and hence this release) has come to have special poignancy in retrospect, as the final live performance from Clarkin and, in all probability, the band itself.

Live Videos/DVDs
The Sacred Hour (1985, Video)
This video is taken from the Camden Palace gig on 13 May 1985, just over two weeks before the Mayfair concert featured on *The River Sessions*. It's a

truncated setlist that's even heavier on *Storyteller's Night* material (eight of the 12 songs). It's been re-released various times on video and DVD, including as *On A Storyteller's Night* (Video, 1985) and *Live From London* (DVD, 2005)

On The Wings Of Heaven Live (1988, Video/Laserdisc)
If you ignore the laboured storyline of a young fan making his way to the venue, this is the best visual representation of Magnum in concert. Filmed at the Hammersmith Odeon on 25/26 March, on the eve of the release of *Wings Of Heaven*, it features the band at the height of its powers, with a stage set, wardrobe (lots of long black coats and ripped jeans) and sound to match. Some of the performances, such as the epics 'Wild Swan' and 'Don't Wake The Lion' and the ballad 'It Must Have Been Love', are simply superb. For the sake of nostalgia alone, this deserves a modern reissue.

A Winter's Tale (2003; Recorded 1992, DVD)
This is a thoroughly entertaining DVD of the band's hometown gig at Birmingham Town Hall on 22 December 1992. It includes the usual classic 1980s tracks as well as two songs from the recent *Sleepwalking* album (although, interestingly, nothing from its predecessor *Goodnight LA*). There's also an early version of 'On Christmas Day' (that would feature on 1994's *Rock Art*) and a fun rendition of 'We Wish You A Merry Christmas'. This has been re-released in various guises, including on DVD as *Live Legends* and *Live At Birmingham* (both 2004) and on CD as *Live From Birmingham* (2013).

Livin' the Dream (2005, DVD)
This double DVD package focuses on the *On A Storyteller's Night* 20th anniversary tour. The concert is from London's Astoria on 23 April 2005 and includes an initial set of recent releases and classics before the track-by-track run-through of *On A Storyteller's Night*. This is masterful stuff, with the rhythm section of Jimmy Copley and Al Barrow filling the big shoes of Barker and Lowe admirably. The second DVD has lots of interviews, promo videos and a lovely acoustic version of 'The Spirit'.

Compilations
There have been dozens of Magnum compilations. This list focuses only on those with significant, original or interesting material, which tend to be those released by record labels with which the band were associated at the time.

Archive (1993, Jet)
Tracklist: 'Sea Bird', 'Stormbringer', 'Slipping Away', 'Captain America', 'Master Of Disguise', 'Without Your Love', 'Find The Time', 'Everybody Needs', 'Kingdom Of Madness' (1979 Version), 'Lights Burned Out' (Demo), 'The Word' (Orchestral Version), 'True Fine Love'

Chapter And Verse: The Very Best Of Magnum (1993, Polydor)
Tracklist: 'Rockin' Chair', 'Vigilante', 'C'est La Vie', 'Heartbroke And Busted', 'On A Storyteller's Night' (Live), 'Start Talking Love', 'Mama', 'Lonely Night', 'Crying Time', 'Midnight' (Remix), 'It Must Have Been Love', 'Days Of No Trust', 'Just Like An Arrow' (Live), 'When The World Comes Down'

The Gathering (2010, Sanctuary)
This is a five-CD career summary running from the first demos to the 2009 *Into The Valley Of The Moonking* album. It features plenty of rare and difficult-to-get-hold of material, including an audio version of the *On The Wings Of Heaven* set from 26 March 1988 at Hammersmith Odeon, with a couple of tracks omitted and three added.

Evolution (2011, SPV)
Tracklist: 'That Holy Touch', 'Just Like January', 'Brand New Morning', 'Immigrant Son', 'When We Were Younger', 'Out Of The Shadows', 'All My Bridges', 'Blood On Your Barbed Wire Thorns' (All Partially Re-Recorded And Remixed), 'The Visitation', 'Wild Angels', 'The Fall' (New Recording), 'Do You Know Who You Are?' (New Recording)

'The Fall' (5:38)
Centred around an airy Big Country-esque riff, this is a lovely melodic track that sees Magnum steering closer to the mainstream than they've been for many years. The music and the opening 'Maybe tomorrow' line also nod, unconsciously perhaps, to the band's 1980s commercial peak and particularly the stunning B-side 'Maybe Tonight'. James is on particularly fine form here, holding the hurtling rhythm in line and contributing a couple of lively drum fills.

'Do You Know Who You Are?' (6:49)
This is in a similar melodic rock vein. It's another great track with catchy hooks aplenty and a great extended instrumental breakdown. The song's length and the haunting background vocals towards the end suggest that Clarkin may have been working towards a more epic feel that isn't quite realised. But the new recordings more than hold their own on what is a solid representation of the first ten years of Magnum Mk. II.

The Valley Of Tears: The Ballads (2017, SPV)
Tracklist: 'Dream About You' (Remastered), 'Back In Your Arms Again' (Newly Re-Recorded), 'The Valley Of Tears' (Remixed, Remastered), 'Broken Wheel' (Newly Re-Recorded), 'A Face In The Crowd' (Remixed, Remastered), 'Your Dreams Won't Die' (Remastered), 'Lonely Night' (Acoustic Version, Newly Re-Recorded), 'The Last Frontier' (Remixed, Remastered), 'Putting Things In Place' (Remixed, Remastered), 'When The World Comes Down' (New Live Version)

Dance Of The Black Tattoo (2021, SPV)

Tracklist: 'Black Skies' (Live), 'Freedom Day' (Live), 'All My Bridges' (Live), 'On A Storyteller's Night' (Live), 'Dance Of The Black Tattoo' (Live), 'On Christmas Day' (2014 Version, Radio Edit), 'Born To Be King' (2014 Version), 'Phantom Of Paradise Circus', 'No God Or Saviour', 'Your Dreams Won't Die' (Live), 'Twelve Men Wise And Just' (Live), 'Show Me Your Hands' (Radio Edit), 'Not Forgiven' (Radio Edit), 'Madman Or Messiah' (Radio Edit)

Bibliography

Books And Journal Articles

Anthony, M., *Words And Music: Excursions In The Art Of Rock Fandom* (Celtic Mist, 2012)

Earl, B., 'The reformer's charter: setting Bloom's *Anxiety Of Influence* in the context of melodic rock', *Popular Music*, 29:1 (2010), 131-142

Earl, B., 'Metal Goes "Pop": The Explosion of Heavy Metal into the Mainstream', in Gerd Beyer (ed.), *Heavy Metal Music In Britain* (Routledge, 2016).

Hornsby, L., *Brum Rocked On!* (GSM Best Sellers, 2003)

Matthews, R., *In Search Of Forever* (Paper Tiger, 1985)

Matthews, R., *Countdown To Millennium* (Paper Tiger, 1997)

Metzer, D., 'The power ballad', *Popular Music*, 31:3 (2012), 437-459

Scott Morgan, D. *Patterns In The Chaos* (Lifeware, 2012)

Stanway, M., *Close To The Mark: Nearly 40 Years Of Behind The Scenes Fun & Madness* (Stanbo, 2015)

Newspapers And Magazines

Birmingham Evening Mail, 1978, 1983, 1985-1986, 1988-1989, 1991, 1996
Birmingham Post, 1983, 1985, 1993
Burton Daily Mail, 1979, 1988
Chester Chronicle, 1994
Classic Rock, 2002, 2005, 2011, 2013-2014, 2020, 2022
Electronics And Music Magazine, 1984
Evening Sentinel, 1983-1984
Fireworks, 2011, 2020, 2022
Guitarist, 2002
Home And Studio Recording, 1987
HRH Rock Mag, Volume 4, 2018
Kerrang!, 1982-1983, 1985-1986, 1988, 1990-1992, 1994
Metal Hammer, 1986, 1988-1990
Newcastle Chronicle, 1986, 1988
Raw, 1988, 1990
Record Collector, 1990, 2022
Record Mirror, 1979, 1980
Rock Candy, 2017, 2021
Sound On Sound, 1989
Sounds, 1978-1979, 1982, 1986
Wondrous Stories: The Journal Of The Classic Rock Society, 1995

Online Resources

magnumonline.co.uk – the official Magnum website
Martin Vielhaber's *The Story Of Magnum*, *magnum-biography.jimdofree.com* – a detailed online history of the band

markstanway.co.uk – the website of Magnum's former keyboard player
getreadyrockradio.com – plenty of Magnum reviews and other material from across the years, including in relation to 'Magnum Month' in March 2022

On Track series
Allman Brothers Band – Andrew Wild 978-1-78952-252-5
Tori Amos – Lisa Torem 978-1-78952-142-9
Aphex Twin – Beau Waddell 978-1-78952-267-9
Asia – Peter Braidis 978-1-78952-099-6
Badfinger – Robert Day-Webb 978-1-878952-176-4
Barclay James Harvest – Keith and Monica Domone 978-1-78952-067-5
Beck – Arthur Lizie 978-1-78952-258-7
The Beatles – Andrew Wild 978-1-78952-009-5
The Beatles Solo 1969-1980 – Andrew Wild 978-1-78952-030-9
Blue Oyster Cult – Jacob Holm-Lupo 978-1-78952-007-1
Blur – Matt Bishop 978-178952-164-1
Marc Bolan and T.Rex – Peter Gallagher 978-1-78952-124-5
Kate Bush – Bill Thomas 978-1-78952-097-2
Camel – Hamish Kuzminski 978-1-78952-040-8
Captain Beefheart – Opher Goodwin 978-1-78952-235-8
Caravan – Andy Boot 978-1-78952-127-6
Cardiacs – Eric Benac 978-1-78952-131-3
Nick Cave and The Bad Seeds – Dominic Sanderson 978-1-78952-240-2
Eric Clapton Solo – Andrew Wild 978-1-78952-141-2
The Clash – Nick Assirati 978-1-78952-077-4
Elvis Costello and The Attractions – Georg Purvis 978-1-78952-129-0
Crosby, Stills and Nash – Andrew Wild 978-1-78952-039-2
Creedence Clearwater Revival – Tony Thompson 978-178952-237-2
The Damned – Morgan Brown 978-1-78952-136-8
Deep Purple and Rainbow 1968-79 – Steve Pilkington 978-1-78952-002-6
Dire Straits – Andrew Wild 978-1-78952-044-6
The Doors – Tony Thompson 978-1-78952-137-5
Dream Theater – Jordan Blum 978-1-78952-050-7
Eagles – John Van der Kiste 978-1-78952-260-0
Earth, Wind and Fire – Bud Wilkins 978-1-78952-272-3
Electric Light Orchestra – Barry Delve 978-1-78952-152-8
Emerson Lake and Palmer – Mike Goode 978-1-78952-000-2
Fairport Convention – Kevan Furbank 978-1-78952-051-4
Peter Gabriel – Graeme Scarfe 978-1-78952-138-2
Genesis – Stuart MacFarlane 978-1-78952-005-7
Gentle Giant – Gary Steel 978-1-78952-058-3
Gong – Kevan Furbank 978-1-78952-082-8
Green Day – William E. Spevack 978-1-78952-261-7
Hall and Oates – Ian Abrahams 978-1-78952-167-2
Hawkwind – Duncan Harris 978-1-78952-052-1
Peter Hammill – Richard Rees Jones 978-1-78952-163-4
Roy Harper – Opher Goodwin 978-1-78952-130-6

Jimi Hendrix – Emma Stott 978-1-78952-175-7
The Hollies – Andrew Darlington 978-1-78952-159-7
Horslips – Richard James 978-1-78952-263-1
The Human League and The Sheffield Scene –
Andrew Darlington 978-1-78952-186-3
The Incredible String Band – Tim Moon 978-1-78952-107-8
Iron Maiden – Steve Pilkington 978-1-78952-061-3
Joe Jackson – Richard James 978-1-78952-189-4
Jefferson Airplane – Richard Butterworth 978-1-78952-143-6
Jethro Tull – Jordan Blum 978-1-78952-016-3
Elton John in the 1970s – Peter Kearns 978-1-78952-034-7
Billy Joel – Lisa Torem 978-1-78952-183-2
Judas Priest – John Tucker 978-1-78952-018-7
Kansas – Kevin Cummings 978-1-78952-057-6
The Kinks – Martin Hutchinson 978-1-78952-172-6
Korn – Matt Karpe 978-1-78952-153-5
Led Zeppelin – Steve Pilkington 978-1-78952-151-1
Level 42 – Matt Philips 978-1-78952-102-3
Little Feat – Georg Purvis - 978-1-78952-168-9
Aimee Mann – Jez Rowden 978-1-78952-036-1
Joni Mitchell – Peter Kearns 978-1-78952-081-1
The Moody Blues – Geoffrey Feakes 978-1-78952-042-2
Motorhead – Duncan Harris 978-1-78952-173-3
Nektar – Scott Meze – 978-1-78952-257-0
New Order – Dennis Remmer – 978-1-78952-249-5
Nightwish – Simon McMurdo – 978-1-78952-270-9
Laura Nyro – Philip Ward 978-1-78952-182-5
Mike Oldfield – Ryan Yard 978-1-78952-060-6
Opeth – Jordan Blum 978-1-78-952-166-5
Pearl Jam – Ben L. Connor 978-1-78952-188-7
Tom Petty – Richard James 978-1-78952-128-3
Pink Floyd – Richard Butterworth 978-1-78952-242-6
The Police – Pete Braidis 978-1-78952-158-0
Porcupine Tree – Nick Holmes 978-1-78952-144-3
Queen – Andrew Wild 978-1-78952-003-3
Radiohead – William Allen 978-1-78952-149-8
Rancid – Paul Matts 989-1-78952-187-0
Renaissance – David Detmer 978-1-78952-062-0
REO Speedwagon – Jim Romag 978-1-78952-262-4
The Rolling Stones 1963-80 – Steve Pilkington 978-1-78952-017-0
The Smiths and Morrissey – Tommy Gunnarsson 978-1-78952-140-5
Spirit – Rev. Keith A. Gordon – 978-1-78952- 248-8
Stackridge – Alan Draper 978-1-78952-232-7

Also available from Sonicbond

Status Quo the Frantic Four Years – Richard James 978-1-78952-160-3
Steely Dan – Jez Rowden 978-1-78952-043-9
Steve Hackett – Geoffrey Feakes 978-1-78952-098-9
Tears For Fears – Paul Clark - 978-178952-238-9
Thin Lizzy – Graeme Stroud 978-1-78952-064-4
Tool – Matt Karpe 978-1-78952-234-1
Toto – Jacob Holm-Lupo 978-1-78952-019-4
U2 – Eoghan Lyng 978-1-78952-078-1
UFO – Richard James 978-1-78952-073-6
Van Der Graaf Generator – Dan Coffey 978-1-78952-031-6
Van Halen – Morgan Brown – 9781-78952-256-3
The Who – Geoffrey Feakes 978-1-78952-076-7
Roy Wood and the Move – James R Turner 978-1-78952-008-8
Yes – Stephen Lambe 978-1-78952-001-9
Frank Zappa 1966 to 1979 – Eric Benac 978-1-78952-033-0
Warren Zevon – Peter Gallagher 978-1-78952-170-2
10CC – Peter Kearns 978-1-78952-054-5

Decades Series
The Bee Gees in the 1960s – Andrew Mon Hughes et al 978-1-78952-148-1
The Bee Gees in the 1970s – Andrew Mon Hughes et al 978-1-78952-179-5
Black Sabbath in the 1970s – Chris Sutton 978-1-78952-171-9
Britpop – Peter Richard Adams and Matt Pooler 978-1-78952-169-6
Phil Collins in the 1980s – Andrew Wild 978-1-78952-185-6
Alice Cooper in the 1970s – Chris Sutton 978-1-78952-104-7
Alice Cooper in the 1980s – Chris Sutton 978-1-78952-259-4
Curved Air in the 1970s – Laura Shenton 978-1-78952-069-9
Donovan in the 1960s – Jeff Fitzgerald 978-1-78952-233-4
Bob Dylan in the 1980s – Don Klees 978-1-78952-157-3
Brian Eno in the 1970s – Gary Parsons 978-1-78952-239-6
Faith No More in the 1990s – Matt Karpe 978-1-78952-250-1
Fleetwood Mac in the 1970s – Andrew Wild 978-1-78952-105-4
Fleetwood Mac in the 1980s – Don Klees 978-178952-254-9
Focus in the 1970s – Stephen Lambe 978-1-78952-079-8
Free and Bad Company in the 1970s – John Van der Kiste 978-1-78952-178-8
Genesis in the 1970s – Bill Thomas 978178952-146-7
George Harrison in the 1970s – Eoghan Lyng 978-1-78952-174-0
Kiss in the 1970s – Peter Gallagher 978-1-78952-246-4
Manfred Mann's Earth Band in the 1970s – John Van der Kiste 978178952-243-3
Marillion in the 1980s – Nathaniel Webb 978-1-78952-065-1
Van Morrison in the 1970s – Peter Childs - 978-1-78952-241-9
Mott the Hoople and Ian Hunter in the 1970s –
John Van der Kiste 978-1-78-952-162-7

Pink Floyd In The 1970s – Georg Purvis 978-1-78952-072-9
Suzi Quatro in the 1970s – Darren Johnson 978-1-78952-236-5
Queen in the 1970s – James Griffiths 978-1-78952-265-5
Roxy Music in the 1970s – Dave Thompson 978-1-78952-180-1
Slade in the 1970s – Darren Johnson 978-1-78952-268-6
Status Quo in the 1980s – Greg Harper 978-1-78952-244-0
Tangerine Dream in the 1970s – Stephen Palmer 978-1-78952-161-0
The Sweet in the 1970s – Darren Johnson 978-1-78952-139-9
Uriah Heep in the 1970s – Steve Pilkington 978-1-78952-103-0
Van der Graaf Generator in the 1970s – Steve Pilkington 978-1-78952-245-7
Rick Wakeman in the 1970s – Geoffrey Feakes 978-1-78952-264-8
Yes in the 1980s – Stephen Lambe with David Watkinson 978-1-78952-125-2

On Screen series
Carry On… – Stephen Lambe 978-1-78952-004-0
David Cronenberg – Patrick Chapman 978-1-78952-071-2
Doctor Who: The David Tennant Years – Jamie Hailstone 978-1-78952-066-8
James Bond – Andrew Wild 978-1-78952-010-1
Monty Python – Steve Pilkington 978-1-78952-047-7
Seinfeld Seasons 1 to 5 – Stephen Lambe 978-1-78952-012-5

Other Books
1967: A Year In Psychedelic Rock 978-1-78952-155-9
1970: A Year In Rock – John Van der Kiste 978-1-78952-147-4
1973: The Golden Year of Progressive Rock 978-1-78952-165-8
Babysitting A Band On The Rocks – G.D. Praetorius 978-1-78952-106-1
Eric Clapton Sessions – Andrew Wild 978-1-78952-177-1
Derek Taylor: For Your Radioactive Children –
Andrew Darlington 978-1-78952-038-5
The Golden Road: The Recording History of The Grateful Dead – John
Kilbride 978-1-78952-156-6
Iggy and The Stooges On Stage 1967-1974 – Per Nilsen 978-1-78952-101-6
Jon Anderson and the Warriors – the road to Yes –
David Watkinson 978-1-78952-059-0
Magic: The David Paton Story – David Paton 978-1-78952-266-2
Misty: The Music of Johnny Mathis – Jakob Baekgaard 978-1-78952-247-1
Nu Metal: A Definitive Guide – Matt Karpe 978-1-78952-063-7
Tommy Bolin: In and Out of Deep Purple – Laura Shenton 978-1-78952-070-5
Maximum Darkness – Deke Leonard 978-1-78952-048-4
The Twang Dynasty – Deke Leonard 978-1-78952-049-1

and many more to come!